To ████████

I am glad we re-connected after so many years. I think you are a wonderful person with a very bright future!!!,

— Dr. Abdalla Roshdy Fam

DELINQUENT
TO
DOCTOR

DELINQUENT

TO

DOCTOR

EMANCIPATION THROUGH EDUCATION AND
EXPOSURE

DR. ABDALLA RASHAD TAU

The Exposure Foundation, Inc.

Edited by Moja Editing, Inc.
Graphic Design by Triumphant Multimedia, www.trimultimedia.com
Web Development and Design by Perfect 10

Library of Congress Control Number: 2012930209

ISBN-13: 978-0-615-55244-6
ISBN-10: 0-615-55244-7

Printed in USA by The Exposure Foundation, Inc. Publishing.

To my parents Bobby and Carolyn Rosemond.

CONTENTS

A NOTE FROM DR. TAU

Delinquent to Doctor chronicles my delinquent adolescent years, as well as my transition into a progressive adult. All experiences and events detailed are factual, and have been documented as I recall them. Names, identities, and circumstances have been modified in order to protect the integrity and/or privacy of the various individuals involved.

DELINQUENT
TO
DOCTOR

The Serenity Prayer

God grant me the serenity

to accept the things I cannot

change;

courage to change the things I

can;

and wisdom to know the

difference.

-Anonymous

INTRODUCTION

DELINQUENT BEHAVIOR

My life has been a very fascinating journey thus far. I have always been an individual that preferred to do things my way. Some people would say that I "march to the beat of my own drum," and it seems like I always know what my next move is going to be. That has not always been the case. Even though I didn't always make the right choices, I pride myself on learning from my mistakes. I've also learned from others' mistakes and in most cases, accepted constructive criticism from my peers. This philosophy has assisted me with achieving any goal I set for myself, but it was by no means easy.

Whenever I tell various stories from my delinquent past, I often preface each story by saying, "This may sound like I am making this up, but I promise to God, I'm not." Once I finish the story, people ask, "How did you change?" I've asked myself the same question many times.

When I reflect on my life and look at how I used to be, the choices I have made, and where I am now, it amazes me. I've realized people make life more challenging than it has to be. I didn't understand that until now. My memories often take me back to my adolescent years, and I wonder how I escaped many of the negative proverbial trappings of life that many black males face. How did I avoid the horrific realities of being a high school dropout, drug addiction, unemployment, incarceration, and early death? Why am I in the minority, not the majority? Who am I? What makes me different? I clearly flirted with those negative outcomes, by virtue of the choices I used to make! Before I address these questions, let's examine why a person displays delinquent behavior from a theoretical perspective.

Theoretical Framework

Delinquent behavior is defined as an overall lack of adherence to the social mores and standards that allow members of a society to exist peaceably (Heckert & Heckert, 2004). Delinquent behavior is multidimensional in nature and cannot be explained with using one theory alone. My delinquent behavior can be explained by understanding the theories of Hirschi (1969) and Merton (1938). Hirschi introduced the Social Control Theory, which does not attempt to explain why individuals indulge in delinquent behavior, but rather why there is noncompliance with conventional norms. Hirschi stated that the attachment an individual has with persons, groups, or institutions (that maintain conventional norms and values) is of central interest. The fragileness of these attachments may possibly breed delinquent behavior. The Theory of Social Control emphasizes the family as the main reference group for a young person and the primary source of attachment.

Social Control Theory

According to Alder et al. (2007), the Social Control Theory states that people display delinquent behavior when they have not internalized the tenets of the social order, have not participated in and committed to conventional activities, and have not established satisfactory attachments. The crux of the Social Control Theory consists of strategies and techniques that control human behavior and lead to obedience and conformity to beliefs about government, the influences of family and school, religious beliefs, friends, moral values, and the laws of society (Alder et al.). Adler et al. also emphasized that the more an individual is committed and obedient to values, conventional activities, and the greater the attachments to loved ones, friends, and parents, the less likely that individual will indulge in delinquent activities. Hirschi proposed that four social bonds promote conformity and socialization. These social bonds consist of attachment, commitment, involvement, and belief (Wagner et al., 2004).

Attachment. According to Wagner et al. (2004), children's emotional attachments to significant people influence the behavior and expectations of the children. Therefore, strong relationships with significant individuals in a child's life should impede the occurrence of delinquent behavior. The family constitutes the main reference group for children, as noted by the Social Control Theory

(Donnelly & Straus, 2005). The Social Control Theory consists of three major forms of attachment, which are: parental control, teachers, and peers. Wagner et al. identified three types of parental control: (a) the form of supervision children receive from the parents, (b) the type of discipline the children receive, and (c) the level of emotional attachment the children have with the parents. If the supervision is nonexistent, discipline is inconsistent, and the emotional attachment is low between the parents and the child, the degree of delinquency increases. The degree of delinquency also increases when children have a low emotional attachment with teachers. Finally, peers as an agent for socialization could not only influence adolescents to achieve social wealth and recognition through means of vocational training and conventional school education, but also influence students to delve into delinquent behavior.

Commitment. The commitment of individuals to invest in life and career goals strengthens the rational consideration for students not to entertain delinquent behavior and lean more toward pursuing conventional goals (Alder et al., 2007). The costs of delinquent behavior (e.g., poor school grades, repeating a school year, etc.) are greater than the gains (e.g., less homework, increased leisure time, etc.), with the high investment in one's educational career. Notwithstanding, if a child accepts failure easily, being permanently delinquent may seem rational as opposed to having a good relationship with the school and the family and having exceptional grades. Various schools have different educational prospects for the career goals of their students. Wagner et al. (2004) reported a correlation between a student's educational career and opportunities a student obtains. This information is very advantageous when measuring why children display delinquent behavior. Donnelly and Straus (2005) suggested that students are less likely to be delinquent if the students have invested an ample amount of time in their educational career.

Involvement. Hirschi (1969) stated that an adolescent's involvement in extracurricular activities decreases the opportunity and amount of time the child has to display delinquent behavior. In addition, the concept of time is related to identifying with conventional values and norms, meaning that the more frequently youth participate in conventional activities, the more they will identify with the activities. Ultimately, an increase in children's positive participation with out-of-school activities decreases children's chances to commit delinquent behavior.

Belief. Hirschi's (1969) fourth social bond of conformity and socialization is belief. Donnelly and Straus (2005) emphasized that strong movement toward conventional norms and beliefs that have been digested in the development of socialization minimizes the recognition of delinquent behavior. Wagner et al. (2004) suggested that the examination of the relationship involving delinquency and the correlation of various risk factors contributing to a permanent career of crime is a testament to the effectiveness of a general campaign toward conventional beliefs and norms. Eventually, the stronger the implementation of conventional beliefs and norms, the more likely delinquent behavior will not transpire.

Anomie Theory

Merton's Anomie Theory builds upon the work of Emile Durkheim. Durkheim's theory was regarded as an analytical framework designated especially for delinquent behavior (Merton, 1938). Durkheim's theory as related to the Anomie Theory attempts to explain different levels of delinquency over various social structures. Merton adopted Durkheim's origin of anomie and further defined it as the incorporation of goals defined by the culture and the institutionalized standards to accomplish these goals (Wagner, Dunkake, & Weiss, 2004). The Anomie Theory is based on the distribution of delinquent behavior among the positions in a social system. The theory seeks to account for differences in the distribution and rates of delinquent behavior among systems.

According to Alder et al. (2007), Durkheim first introduced the concept of anomie in 1893, defining anomie as a collapse in social order because of a loss of values and standards. The concept of the Anomie Theory dates back to Greek philosophy, which emerged from a Greek word that describes lawlessness (Heckert & Heckert, 2004). Durkheim's theory of anomie states that crime in society is as common as birth and death and the justification of human conduct dwells in social organizations and groups (Messner

& Rosenfeld, 2001). Durkheim suggested that as society expands, the universal set of rules evolve, groups become divided, and the expectations and actions of one group are adverse to opposition groups.

According to Featherstone and Deflem (2003), Merton borrowed the term anomie from Durkheim to describe the fact that society is composed of equal goals for all its members, without providing equal opportunities to achieve goals. Individuals who cannot achieve these goals using conventional means may opt to use delinquent modes to achieve their objective (Passas, 2000). Tittle and Paternoster (2000) reported that the Anomie Theory is often referred to as a discrepancy in cultural goals and the lawful means to attain these goals. Specifically, anomie exists when people deviate from societal rules to achieve personal goals (Featherstone & Deflem). Overall, the Anomie Theory is concerned with the incongruent emphasis between cultural goals and institutional means. Wagner et al. (2004) described five potential individual reactions for the pull between institutionalized means and cultural goals and their correlation with delinquent behavior. These reactions are conformity, innovation, ritualism, retreatism, and rebellion.

Conformity. Conformity is the attainment of legitimate goals through legitimate means, which is considered a normal reaction within a stable society (Broidy, 2001). The individual who makes the decision to conform has internalized the concept of why and how success in life is linked to cultural goals and possesses legitimate means required to attain these goals; thus delinquency does not transpire in this situation. Nonetheless, Merton (1938) had an interest in the various adaptations an individual could display. Merton wanted to know the extent to which conditions influenced the social structure to cause a particular delinquent behavior (Passas, 2000).

Innovation. Wagner et al. (2004) also suggested that Merton's second type of adaptation of innovation appears if an individual aspires to achieve cultural goals but has limited access to legitimate means. Individuals who are deemed members of the lower social class exemplify innovation in that these individuals do not posses legitimate means of acquiring economic wealth, which increases their chances of incorporating unconventional means to reach their goals, such as robbery, gambling, prostitution, larceny, drug dealing, and theft.

Ritualism. Ritualism is considered a delinquent behavior in a restrictive sense because the goals adjust to the means (Bernburg, 2002). Ritualists tend to recognize the legitimate means, but do not aspire to achieve the goals defined by the culture, particularly concerning social acceptance and economic stability. An example of this behavior is a child that attends class everyday, brings all their materials, doesn't create any disruptions, seems to be paying attention, but never completes any assignments and ultimately fails the class.

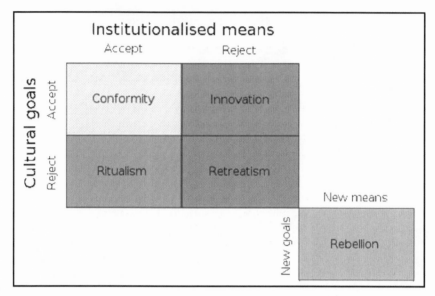

Robert Merton's Deviance Typology.

Retreatism. Merton (1938) stated that individuals who display the adaptation of retreatism, such as social outcasts, either abstain or simply refuse to adhere to the quest for legitimate means and goals. Common characteristics of negative retreatism are underconformity to both cultural goals and legitimate means coupled with negative social reactions. Examples of negative retreatism are hermits, polygamist Mormons, the homeless, hobos, Jehovah's Witnesses, and substance abusers.

Rebellion. Negative rebellion constitutes an exceptional adaptation, because negative rebellion involves a condition or behavior where there is nonconformity to goals and rules, while attempting to substitute new goals and rules, and a negative social reaction. Examples of negative rebellion include betraying national secrets, flag defilement, revolutionary behavior that is negatively evaluated, advocating contrary government philosophy, giving up citizenship, and treason. Specific examples are separatist groups, freedom fighters, and survivalist groups. While formulating the Theory of Anomie to explain delinquent behavior, Merton also established the Strain Theory.

Strain Theory

Merton's (1938) second theory is the Strain Theory of delinquency. Current Strain Theory states that delinquency results from the obstruction of goal-seeking behavior (Agnew, 2001). The foundation of Strain Theory is based on the idea that the inability to achieve goals through legitimate channels breeds delinquency. Delinquency emerges when an individual disobeys the standards of the social group (Heckert & Heckert, 2004). Merton stated that delinquent behavior refers to conduct that deviates from the standards set for people according to social status. As a result, individuals may possibly look to illicit means of achieving goals or attack the source of any perceived agitation or resentment (Alder et al., 2007).

Through self examination, I do not feel the Social Control Theory adequately explains my delinquent behavior because my social bonds were mostly strong. However, when I was not involved in something constructive, I became bored. I believe that is when I participated in most of my delinquent activities. According to Anomie Theory, my reactions to institutionalized means and cultural goals in a Euro-society were conformity or rebellion, depending on the circumstances. I have never been the type of person who accepts something at face value. I must have a rhyme and a reason. According to my parents, I was this way from birth. How did I go from a delinquent to a doctor? This is a precautionary tale with a positive outcome.

MOJA

THE EARLY YEARS

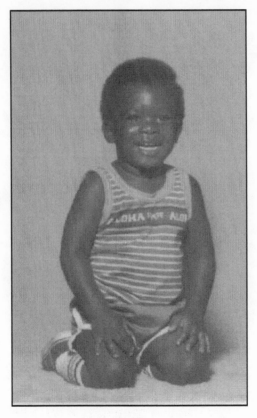

Age 2.

I entered the world as Mack Rashad Rosemond on February 3, 1977 in Albany, Georgia to Bobby Lee Rosemond and Carolyn Williams Rosemond. My father grew up in Seneca, South

Carolina, and my mother grew up in Abbeville, Alabama. Neither of my paternal or maternal grandparents married nor had education beyond the primary years. However, my parents both attended and graduated from Albany State University, where they met and have been married for thirty-nine years. Both have acquired degrees, licenses and certifications on the graduate level. Needless to say, their belief in education was very strong and it was understood early that I was to be educated as well.

With my sister Tonae at the King Center.

I have an older sister, Tonae, and a younger brother, Maurice. I was never really close to other family members outside of my immediate family. I was somewhat close to my maternal grandfather, although we did not see each other often. My maternal

2

grandmother was not very affectionate towards us. I met my paternal grandfather once and he died shortly thereafter. I was the closest to my paternal grandmother.

Kindergarten Class Photo.

My Personality

People often ask me where I got my personality from. My parents explain that I always had my own thoughts about life and about how things should and should not be. I feel that I am 10% my father, 10% my mother, and 80% me. My revolutionary thoughts, business sense, and cut-throat mentality is my father. My need to always be involved in something, the inability to sit still, and being an extravert are characteristic of my mother. I was a very inquisitive child that always asked, "Why?"

With my little brother Maurice.

My mother says I have been "head strong" since I was fifteen months of age. As a baby, my mother attempted to introduce me to different types of foods such as carrots, but I would not and did not want to deviate from what I was already accustomed too. She would try to feed me carrots and I would say, "I don't nike it" (baby talk). In elementary school I refused to wear long sleeves during the winter months and I was adamant about not wearing shorts in the summer months. No one could ever tell me or make me do something or give me information without an explanation. I always asked, "Why? Why? Why?" until I was satisfied. As a child my incessant questions landed me in a lot of trouble, but it also helped me academically. Academics were always a major theme in the Rosemond household. But along with academics, my parents kept my brother and I involved in various extracurricular activities.

As far back as the age of four, I remember going to swim class and gymnastics practice. I participated in football during the fall, basketball in the winter, and baseball in the spring and summer. In addition to sports, I was also involved in the cub scouts, and boy scouts. My parents believed that keeping their children involved with positive activities would breed success and help to minimize delinquent behaviors that Black males in America fall victim too. For the most part, I took care of business academically and my behavior was mediocre. I enjoyed all aspects of my childhood, except for one thing; I hated being black and my dark skinned black complexion.

Black Boy

I vividly recall being teased about my dark black skin. I was called every phrase that existed in the English language that began with the word Black (e.g., black boy, black dog, black smut, black ass, ol' black ass nigger.......). It was not very fashionable to be dark skinned in the '80s. I can even remember having a

5

conversation with my mother when I was about nine or ten about my behavior and why I was acting out. At a point I started crying and I said, "Everybody hates me because I am black." I hate to admit this, but if I could have gone to a beauty supply store to purchase a chemical to make me European-looking or light-skinned, I would have jumped at the chance. I did not have the luxury to change my skin like sisters who could change their tightly coiled hair to straight. I know now that my self-hatred was attributed to having a "slave mentality."

Slave Mentality

A slave is a person owned by another, forced into performing free labor. Mentality is basically a way of thinking. In the case of present-day Africans in the Americas (North and South America, and the Caribbean), whose descendants were kidnapped by Europeans, thrown in the belly of ships, and then held in complete servitude, the slave mentality is still prevalent. Africans were supposed to be completely subservient to the same early Europeans who exterminated the Native Americans and stole their land. I guess they didn't have enough testicular fortitude to create a nation on their own.

Plantation System

The slave mentality was the result of European colonialism and the plantation system enforced throughout the African Diaspora by the slave traders. A Caribbean slave master named Willie Lynch coined the phrase "making a slave" which implanted the slave mentality into the minds and spirits of my forefathers. The slave owners replaced their African names with European names and brutally enforced speaking only European languages, practicing Christianity, and stripped them of every aspect of their African culture. The ultimate purpose was to divide, conquer, and control the minds, spirits, and bodies of African slaves. The Europeans figured if they could control a man's mind and spirit, they could control his body. If implemented correctly, this recipe for slavery was guaranteed to last for four centuries.

One can argue that Willie Lynch's concept of slavery is still in effect mentally, spiritually, and physically in today's society. I also subscribed to the slave mentality and plantation system by exhibiting self-hatred and embracing everything European including Christianity and celebrating European holidays. My behavior as a delinquent during adolescence and beyond is a direct result. At the age of fourteen the journey to get my spirit and mind back and the chipping away of my slave mentality began.

MBILI

SMELLING MYSELF

As mentioned previously, being teased about my dark skin caused my self esteem to be low. I was also very shy, which many people that know me presently do not believe. I could not even articulate how I felt about a female that I was interested in, or even talk in front of my peers. My shyness lasted all the way to high school. During the summer of 1991, the summer before 9th grade, things started to change.

Summer Job

That summer, I made a decision to start taking control of my life. I don't remember if this was a conscious or unconscious decision. Nevertheless, I believed it was time to make a change. That summer I was fourteen and I was qualified to be employed. My father was in the Army National Guard, so my family had access to military installations, specifically military grocery stores or commissaries. The commissaries had two types of employment for individuals like myself: cashier or bagger. Baggers bagged groceries and took the items to the car for monetary tips. My mother knew some of the individuals that worked at the commissary and was able to get me a position as a bagger.

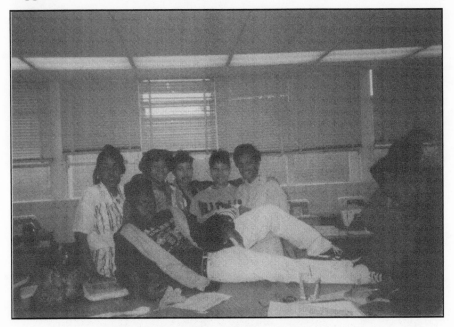

Hanging out in the Home Economics room.

Initially, during the school year I would only work a couple of evenings per week. During the summer I worked everyday including Sundays. I did not mind, because I wanted to make my own money thus being able to make financial choices independent of my parents. One main financial decision I wanted to have control over was purchasing my own clothes. Up until that point, my parents purchased my clothes, which meant I had to accept whatever they purchased. I think I was looking for a little more autonomy. This job afforded me that opportunity. I worked all summer and I saved a significant amount of money.

DELINQUENT TO DOCTOR

First Day of School (9th Grade)

In the early '90s, the most fashionable things to wear were Air Jordan's, Rayon Shirts, and sports wear by a company called Starter. Male hairdos at that time were called "boxes," "pee-wees," "high rights," and "slopes." I purposely did not cut my hair all summer to grow it out, so that I could have the perfect box when school started. With the money I earned, I saved most of it and also went shopping for my own clothes for the first time. I purchased a pair of Air Jordan's, six Rayon shirts, six pair of Lee jeans, a Red Sox baseball jersey, a bottle of Eternity cologne, a gold ring, and a gold rope chain with a gold crown charm. I believed I was set for the first day of school, but still a bit apprehensive.

The first day of school came and I got a very positive response from various classmates. I remember a comment in particular that a female made to a friend of mine.

"Who is that?" she asked.

"That's Rashad," my homeboy responded.

"He really came up over the summer!"

This was also the time females started commenting on my dark skin in a positive way, which was a complete 180 from the comments in the past. I began to hear, "You are so sexy and black," "Sexual chocolate," and most common was "you are cute to be dark-skinned."

Cute to be Dark-skinned

Now, I didn't know if this statement was a comment or an insult. I guess it can be qualified as part comment, part insult. On one hand, females were commenting on my physical appearance in a positive way, but at the same time perpetuating a negative, stereotypical claim that if you were a light-skinned African, you were superior to a dark-skinned African. This concept originated on the slave plantation, where the light-skinned Africans, who were sometimes offspring of the slave master and female African slaves, generally worked and resided in or very near to the master's house. Meanwhile, the dark-skinned slaves worked in the fields and lived in the barn with the livestock.

Until the late '80s and early '90s, being a light-skinned black person was the most accepted in America. The most popular African sex symbols at that time were Prince, Michael Jackson, Apollonia, Vanity, Sheila E, Christopher Williams, Al B Sure, and El DeBarge, just to name a few. Many females at the time always wanted a boyfriend with "good hair" and many of the guys were using S-Curl, Hawaiian Silky, and Duke hair texturizers to make their hair less coiled including me. Many comedians now joke that being light-skinned is "out of style" and "dark-skin is in" and here to stay because of one man, Wesley Snipes.

Wesley Snipes

Wesley Snipes was a very popular dark-skinned actor in the '90s. He is probably most known for playing Nino Brown in *New*

11

Jack City and a vampire in *Blade*. Wesley Snipes made being dark-skinned cool and seemingly more acceptable. It seemed like every movie he was in, there was a sex scene showing him partially nude. Every time his movies were released, girls would come to school commenting on what they thought about his performance. They would also make comments relating to them finding a dark-skinned brother to kick-it with. Thank you Mr. Wesley Snipes for helping a brother out! Dark-skinned brothers have been in-style ever since.

Started Loosing my Mind

High school was a very happy and exciting time in my life and also when I began to exhibit delinquent behavior. When I started making my own money and became involved with girls, my confidence and ego expanded, while my respect for authority diminished. I increasingly wanted to do things on my terms during my framework of time by any means necessary, which was not always necessarily positive.

I started having sex, hanging out past my curfew, smoking weed and drinking alcohol at the same time. The old folks call this condition, "smelling yourself." For those of you that are not familiar with this jargon, "smelling yourself" is a phrase reserved for individuals that think they know everything and no one can tell them anything. In retrospect, I seemed to be fine when I was involved in extracurricular activities, but when I was not involved, that is when I started experimenting in different realms of deviant behavior. My grandmother used to say, "An idle mind is the devil's workshop," and as an adolescent I found myself falling victim to idleness.

TATU

NEGATIVE SELF-DISCOVERY

My life has always been somewhat of a paradox. When I was in high school, it was most apparent. I was in all advance classes, but all my associates were in conventional classes. I remember when I talked my mother into taking me out of my advance classes. What I really wanted was to be with my friends, but I convinced my mother that I needed to change classes because of my math teacher who I considered a racist. I did have a major issue with him and his class, but that wasn't the real reason I wanted to change. I just wanted O-U-T! Eventually, my mother took me out of the class, which ultimately changed all my classes. The day after my schedule changed, I walked into my new science class, which was with Ms. Joyce Robinson.

Ms. Robinson, now Dr. Robinson, played an intricate part in my present-day success. As soon as I walked in her class, her immediate response was, "Oh no, you are not coming in here, I will not allow it! You are too smart not to be in your advance classes." She immediately took me to the counselor's office to set up a meeting with my parents in order to change my classes *back* to their original status. I appreciate Dr. Robinson for stepping in and assuring that I stayed in my appropriate classes. However, this correction did not impede the process of my delinquent behavior manifesting itself. I began to experiment with drinking alcohol, smoking weed, gambling, and sneaking into nightclubs I was not old enough to patronize, and stealing. I was also shot at twice, and had a gun put in my chest (more about this later).

Drinking

I started experimenting with alcohol at fourteen. In the early '90s the alcohol of choice in my community was MD 20/20 (Mad Dog), Night Train, Thunderbird, Cisco, Gin and Juice, and Malt Liquor just to name a few. Of course I was not old enough to purchase alcohol, but I knew individuals that were old enough to purchase it for me. If my friends and I could not find someone to purchase the alcohol, we would walk in the grocery store and steal it. I was never really a heavy drinker, but I've been drunk. In retrospect, I probably had more bad experiences with drinking than positive experiences. Whether it was vomiting in the bathroom of a night club in Las Vegas, vomiting on the MARTA train on New Year's Eve in 1997, or countless hangovers, drinking became a real drag. I had my share of bad experiences, so I stopped drinking. I have not had a drink in over eight years.

Smoking Weed

I remember the first time I smoked weed as if it was yesterday. I was with my friends Jason, Xavier, Bruce, Anthony, and Eric and we called ourselves "Q-MACK." Q-MACK was an acronym of all our names. The name also represented the fact that we thought we were very popular with the ladies. The name was a combination of GQ (Men's Fashion Magazine) and being a Mack Daddy. I do not remember where we got the weed from, but I remember we were at Jason's mother's house at the kitchen table. The first time I hit the weed I started laughing my butt off. It made me very light-headed and relaxed. We were so high that after we finished smoking all the weed, someone had the bright idea to roll up some leaves from one of Jason's mother's plants. I did not participate in that portion of the weed session, I was not that crazy.

I never really liked smoking and I guess I was more of a social smoker. As a matter of fact, I only smoked weed if females were present. It did not make sense for me to sit around and smoke with a bunch of dudes everyday. I occasionally smoked weed beginning in high school through my college years. Like drinking, I eventually gave up weed and have not smoked since 1997.

Fighting

Fighting was a constant in my school and community. If they did not occur in the neighborhood or at school, you could guarantee that there would be a fight or two (or three, or maybe four) at Golden Glide Skating Rink every Saturday night. It seemed like everyone had to represent their neighborhood by showing how tough they thought they were. The neighborhood that I represented was Emerald Estates. We got into many a brawl

16

together. As I look back on it, we were really stupid. I feel that this behavior was an example of self-hatred. Fighting and jumping people just because they were from a different neighborhood was cowardly and non-progressive. Those fights could also have turned deadly.

Wrong Place Wrong Time

I wasn't always victorious at the end of my bouts. A few times, certain situations escalated to a whole other level. During my high school years, I was shot at three times, twice from a distance and once close up. Each time I was shot at, I was at the wrong place at the wrong time.

First Shooting

The first shooting incident took place off of Moreland Avenue at Club XS. Back then Atlanta had a local dance show called *Atlanta Live*. *Atlanta Live* was a local version of Soul Train or American Band Stand for youth. Many of the teenagers from around the city patronized the club every Tuesday night so that we could be featured dancers on the show. One night I asked my mother to drop my friend and I off, so that we could be on the show.

The entire night was great, until we got into the parking lot and noticed that there was a lot of commotion. Unbeknownst to Eric and I, some of our friends from our neighborhood had just jumped some guy in the parking lot. We did not participate in this particular beat down. After the fight was over, most of the

17

teenagers that patronized the club disbursed, but we were still waiting because my mother was late picking us up.

After waiting a while, we walked across the street to use the pay phone. As I was calling my mother, Eric asked, "Rashad, Rashad, who is that driving around the corner?" All of a sudden we saw a car driving toward us, and it was moving fast. We both were like, "Run! Run!" As we started running in the opposite direction, we heard shots rang out. Pop! Pop! Pop! They were shooting at us as we ran across the street! I actually felt bullets whizzing passed my ears! I was praying that we did not get shot. We made it safely to Kroger, a local grocery store in the area. I was thinking that once we made it inside, we would be safe. However, the guys in the car came in after us! Until we were confronted in the store, I had no idea why these dudes were shooting at us. Then one of the guys said that they were going to "fuck us up" for jumping his cousin. We were about to fight in the store until someone said, "Call the police." The guys then ran out of the store. Wow! Talk about being at the wrong place at the wrong time!

Second Shooting

My second shooting incident was at a house party in Decatur in a neighborhood called Columbia Valley. Some friends and I decided to go to a house party one night. Shortly after arriving, my friends decided to leave, but I wanted to stay. I assumed I would be ok, because I was not far from home. I figured I would find a ride home after.

The party was in the basement of a split level house. I remember it being pitch black and I was dancing with a young lady by a pool table. We were actually in between the pool table and the wall. All of a sudden a group of guys surrounded me and yelled, "Nigga, who are you?" At that moment I went into survival mode and I started swinging at everything and everyone I could hit. Next, I scooped one of the guys up and slammed him through the sliding window screen and we ended up on the back porch. It was the fall season and there were leaves everywhere. As I continued to fight, I slipped on a pile of leaves.

Once I slipped on the leaves, they commenced to whooping my ass. All I felt were size 10s, 11s, and 12s on my back, arms, and legs, because I was curled up in the fetal position. All of a sudden, someone kicked me off the back patio deck onto the ground. Next I heard two gun shots, and I felt leaves popping up in the air around me. I guess the guys that jumped me ran off and I went into the house to call someone to come get me. While I was on the phone, someone noticed a bullet sized hole in the underarm portion of my shirt. I checked myself thoroughly to make sure I was not shot. Luckily, I was in one piece. I had dodged another bullet, pun intended. To this day I don't know why they jumped me. Wow! Wrong place, wrong time... again!

Third Shooting

My last life or death situation was at another house party. My best friend from high school and I were invited to a birthday party

19

by a female we knew from a nearby high school. Once again I found myself at another house party in a basement. It was a cool groove, until all of a sudden we noticed some guys harassing another guy at the party. I am not sure why, but my homeboy and I decided to be good Samaritans and intervene in order to stop the brother from getting hurt. The agitators left. At least we *thought* they left.

The guys came back in the house and one of the guys had a gun. By this time everyone had come upstairs. The guy with the gun came right at me and put the gun in my chest. He asked me if I had anything else to say. I just stood there and starred at him as the gun was pressed into my chest. All of a sudden he pulled the trigger, and my life flashed before my eyes. The sun, moon, and stars must have been aligned that night, because the gun jammed and the guy ran off. Years later, I ran into the same guy that we helped out at a party at Georgia Southern University. When we saw each other, we just busted out laughing and reminisced about that night. Wow! Wrong place and wrong time a third time, but definitely not the last!

Gambling

As an adult, I love visiting Las Vegas regularly, however I hate gambling. I don't bet on sporting events, card games, or any other activities that involve betting money. My disdain for gambling goes back to a trip I took on the MARTA bus one fine day in the early nineties. MARTA is the public transportation system in Atlanta. On this particular day I was on my way downtown to purchase a new pair of tennis shoes from Walter's, a shoe store still located in the original building. I caught the 96 bus en route to Decatur Station. Once I sat down on the bus, I noticed some activity going on in the back. My curiosity got the best of me and I decided to go and investigate the situation. Once I was at the back of the bus I observed a man with a piece of cardboard in his lap with three Karo Syrup bottle tops and a small red ball on top. At the time, I did not know the name of the game. I now understand it was a con game disguised as a shell game.

The man juggled one ball between three tops. The object of the game was for the contestant to find which top contained the ball. The contestant gambled by making a bet, then choosing where they thought the ball was. If they found the ball, their money was doubled, if they lost, they lost their money. As I watched people win five, ten, and twenty dollars, I became very intrigued, and I decided to play.

I started out the gate winning small amounts of money back to back, maybe five or ten dollars. In retrospect I should have quit while I was ahead, but I did not. As a result, not only did I lose all my money, I also lost my newly acquired gold chain, gold crown charm, and gold bracelet. When I reached my destination, I departed from the bus dejected and humiliated.

Later that night, I re-examined what happened to me earlier in the day. As I looked back on the incident, I was trying to figure out how I lost, because I thought I knew where the ball was. Suddenly, I realized that the man was not working alone. At that moment I realized that the two men and one woman that won money in the beginning of the game were conspiring with the man! It was my first and last experience being hustled! To date, I refuse to gamble, because I refuse to be hustled. I feel that if I keep my money in my pocket and refuse to gamble, the possibility of feeling dejected and humiliated is significantly minimized.

Clubbing

I presently don't frequent clubs, either. My mother says that the reason I do not like to go to clubs is that I clubbed early on in my life. That may be a very true statement. Since I associated with older and mature individuals, I tended to participate in older and more mature activities like frequenting nightclubs, strip clubs, and sports bars.

Sharon's Showcase

The first time I attended a night club was the summer of 1991. My friends and I frequented one night club in particular called "Sharon's Showcase." Every Saturday we followed our weekly routine which began at the mall and ended at the club. Our day began on the MARTA bus, which we rode to South DeKalb Mall on Candler Road in Decatur. While at the mall, we would meet girls, go to the movies, and hang out at the arcade. After leaving the mall, we headed to Golden Glide Skating Rink on

Wesley Chapel, also in Decatur. The skating rink closed at 12:00 a.m. Afterwards, we headed to Sharon's Showcase.

Sharon's Showcase was essentially a nightclub for teenagers aged thirteen to twenty. However, it operated like an adult nightclub. Sharon's Showcase had a full bar with all types of hard liquor and beer. There was illegal sale and consumption of marijuana, and the club had strippers that came out at 3:00 a.m. Many of these girls were underage and some of them attended a high school called Open Campus. Open Campus was for students who were trying to graduate on time but faced various obstacles such as teenage pregnancy, dysfunctional family structures, and incarceration that caused them to lose credits at their home school. To this day, I am not sure how the club lasted so long; it was quite an interesting set-up.

Club XS

The first adult night club I attended was Club XS which was for adults twenty-one and older. However, the security guards had a side hustle of granting underage patrons entry for a nominal fee. I did not mind paying the fee, because I thought I was grown and I wanted to get in. Club XS was also off of Moreland Avenue and one of the host locations of the annual Spring Break gathering that used to take place in Atlanta known as *Freaknik*.

Freaknik

Freaknik was a phenomenon like no other. It was like Woodstock except it took place annually over a span of approximately eight years. I attended Freaknik for the first time in 1993. A couple of friends and I attended the three day long party that year. We spent most of our time off Moreland Avenue and in the parking lot of Club XS. The only reason we did not go into the club was because the line was too long, it cost too much, and we just decided to "parking lot pimp." Parking lot pimping is when males talk to the females they meet in the parking lot.

We were high school students participating in events for college students. A lot of smoking and drinking took place. The party was so out of control that there were traffic jams all over the city. At some points, people would just get out of the car and party in the street. City officials eventually shut it down right before the 1996 Olympics. If you were not able to have this experience, you are out of luck. It was once in a lifetime.

The Strip Club

The first time I attended a strip club, I was fourteen. I remember this experience vividly. It was in the summer of 1991 and my homeboys and I were hanging out in a friend's front yard. Remember, in 1991 I was fourteen preparing for the ninth grade. However, there were a few guys that still associated with us although they had already graduated from high school. On this particular night, one of the guys named Tony approached my friends and I with a suggestion. He had already graduated from our high school in 1989. I believe he was twenty-one at the time. During our conversation, he asked us if we wanted to see something interesting that we had never seen before. We blindly said yes, jumped into three different cars and proceeded towards downtown Atlanta.

We were ten young African males on a blind adventure. After riding down I-20 West for about twenty minutes, we found ourselves in the West End, which is on the Westside of Atlanta. On the first stop of our adventure, we found ourselves at a strip club called "Montrey's," presently called "Queen City." At this point in my life I had never attended a strip club. Of course with us being underage, our main concern was how we were going to get in. Tony said, "Don't worry about it. Just hand the front attendant your money and they will let you in." Sure enough we handed the cashier our money, the security guard frisked us, and we walked right in, as if we were old enough to patronize the establishment. I believe I experienced culture shock.

When I walked in, all I saw was booty, booty, and more booty. This was the very first time that I saw totally nude women up-close and personal. This was also the first time I saw a woman dancing on stage nude, and climbing up and down a pole, while doing various tricks. It was like being at an x-rated circus. I believe I was simultaneously excited and frightened. While at Montrey's, I was also able to purchase alcohol. We stayed at Montrey's for a few hours and it was time to go. Tony told us that we had one more stop to make. We left the West End en route to Stewart Avenue, presently known as Metropolitan Avenue.

❦ DELINQUENT TO DOCTOR

Stewart Avenue

Stewart Avenue was a very seedy area of town. This community was infested with homelessness, drugs, violence, and prostitution. Unbeknownst to us, Tony took us there to solicit prostitutes. This was my second culture shock of the night. The prostitutes on Stewart Avenue worked out of low budget motels. Once we were on Stewart Avenue, we drove through different hotel parking lots looking at the different girls that were walking around with stilettos, synthetic weaves, fake eyelashes, long acrylic fingernails, tattoos, and over applied make-up with no underwear on. How did I know that the women were not wearing underwear? Their dresses were so extremely short that every time they walked, the dresses would rise up making their booty cheeks and vagina visible. Needless to say, my eyeballs were popping out of my head, because I was fourteen, and I had only been intimate with a female twice. At this point I was entertaining the idea of having my third sexual experience with a prostitute, in a seedy motel, on Stewart Avenue.

As I mentioned earlier, I had been working at the commissary bagging groceries and saved a substantial amount of money. Toney, Dexter, and I were all interested in soliciting a prostitute. The price of "tricking off" at that time, for that location was $20 per person. The problem was that I was the only one that had cash on hand, which was a crisp $100 bill. With me being the youngest and most naive of the group, Tony and Dexter coerced me into paying for them with a promise that they would pay me later. To date, I have not received payment.

We all agreed on one girl to temporarily employ. However, she did not have change. In order for me to get change, I had to walk up the hill to another location. At the top of the hill, I found myself looking at this older brother in a very flashy red suit, snake skin cowboy boots, a jheri curl, wide brim hat, rings on every finger, and a lot of jewelry around his neck. In retrospect, this man was the young lady's pimp, but at that time I did not know. I received my change, went back down the hill, and paid the young lady. We each took turns going in to the young woman's room for sexual services. Once we were all finished, we decided to head back to Decatur and called it a night. This was my first and last experience in the world of prostitution.

I consumed alcohol as a minor, smoked marijuana, gambled, patronized nightclubs and strip clubs, and had intercourse with a prostitute. As much as I hate to admit, I was also a thief. My grandfather used to say, "You can never trust a liar or a thief, because if you lie, you will steal, and if you steal, you will kill." Needless to say, I was one step away from committing homicide, figuratively speaking.

Al Bundy

In the late 1980s, I watched a sitcom on the Fox Network, called *Married with Children*. One of the characters on the show was Al Bundy. Al sold women shoes in a mall. I identified with Al.

27

DELINQUENT TO DOCTOR

When I was in high school, I had about twenty-five jobs. One of those jobs was as a shoes salesman at Baker's Shoes in South DeKalb Mall. Baker's Shoes was a female shoe store. I guess you're wondering, why in the world a young African male would want to work in female shoe store. I was simply able to combine two things that I enjoyed the most at the time: talking to girls and making money. I was responsible for selling shoes and accessories and managing weekly shipments of merchandise.

Operating as a salesman came natural to me. I had always loved talking to people, especially females, so working in a women's shoe store was perfect. However, handling shipments was not very exciting. Shipments of shoes and accessories were delivered every Wednesday. I was responsible for verifying the accuracy of all items delivered and making sure that the inventory was stocked according to the stock number on the box or the package in the back of the store that was designated for stock items. Accessories were pretty easy to manage. Stocking the shoes was a slightly more involved process. All shoes were supposed to be stocked along the walls on shelves in rows from the floor to the ceiling. On average, it took me about five hours to verify the accuracy of a shipment, stock items, and discard the boxes the shipment came in. During various holidays, shipments were larger, hence stocking days took longer. It was quite a daunting task. I requested an additional stock person to help me with the shipments, my request was denied.

"You can handle it," my manager assured me.

"Ok," I simply replied.

Thus, my illegal inside operation began.

Let me first say that just because you choose to justify something, does not necessarily make it right. But that is exactly what I did when I started my illegal shoe sales business. I thought, "Since you want to work me like I was on some plantation in antebellum South Carolina, I need retribution" and I got it through stealing and selling shoes on the white market. Since I handled every piece of merchandise that came in and out of the store, the accuracy of stock on hand started and ended with me, but I was smart about it. I made sure I never got greedy and gauged when it was time to quit. I had a very sophisticated operation for a fifteen year old man in training.

When the shoe shipments came in, I would have to verify the style and number of sizes per style. Each style had a certain number of sizes ranging from size five to eleven. I had to maintain a certain level of discretion to avoid drawing suspicion, so I only took a couple of pair of shoes from each box. Stealing all of one style of shoes would possibly draw suspicion, and I never got greedy.

Once I stocked the shipment, I had to discard the boxes and trash. As I unpacked the shipment, I would take one to three pairs of shoes from each box and place them in what I called "my consolidation box." I would take approximately twenty pairs of shoes per shipment. Once I boxed the shoes, I simply integrated the box in with the rest of the boxes and trash and took it all to the dump outside the mall. When I arrived at the dump, I would discard the trash and put the consolidated box of shoes against the dumpster. The process was complete once I paged my accomplice Dexter to indicate that he needed to pick up the box. After work, I went by his house, paid him a pick-up fee, and collected my merchandise. Now I had to push the product!

I priced all the shoes at 50% below listed price because they were hot (stolen) and I wanted to get rid of the merchandise quickly. I sold a great number of shoes to my classmates, but once Dexter's mother and aunt got a look at the merchandise, my clientele rapidly increased. Not only were they my best customers, but Dexter's mother made me an offer I could not resist. She worked in an office with a high population of females. She said she would move the merchandise as long as I provided her with complimentary shoes of her choice. I agreed to her terms, because that was one less thing I had to worry about.

In addition to making money from shoes I took from the shipment, I also made money on the sales floor. When I was in the store working with young ladies who in the process of making a purchase, I had to gauge if they were down for the hook-up. Once I determined they would not snitch on me, I simply made them a deal on the floor. The conditions were that they had to pay me in cash and they could not return the shoes. They came to the counter, I bagged the shoes, they gave me cash, and they were on their way. I was making money "hand over fist." People even started referring to me as Al Bundy, because I was known as the guy who could provide shoes at a discounted price. Due to my success, my discretion started to dissipate, it was time to get out while I was on top, and that is exactly what I did. I quit, thus Al Bundy was dead.

With my childhood friends.

31

NNE

DOPE BOY

During my adolescent years, I got involved in various negative activities because I was bored (As an adult, I *still* have to make sure I stay involved in various constructive and progressive activities). My most delinquent activity was selling illegal narcotics. Now, I want to make it very clear that I was not a big time, major drug dealer. I was definitely not a "Nino Brown."

I was introduced to selling illegal drugs at age fifteen by the brother of a young lady I was dating at the time. He wanted to invest in my friend and me and agreed to front us. "Fronting" meant he provided us the money to buy and sell the drugs and we paid him a share. He gave us $100 to buy crack and marijuana and also gave us an old, beat-up, blue Pinto so that we could get around. We initially purchased a $50 slab and a half ounce of marijuana. At the time, this amount of drugs yielded a $100 profit and another $100 dollars to re-up (buy more drugs).

Old English Inn

Once the car was functional and we cut and bagged the drugs to sell, we had to find a location for distribution (a trap). A trap is a place where a person can purchase and sell drugs. We decided on the Old English Inn, a motel off Glenwood Road and Highway 285, in Decatur. In the summer of 1992, we were at the motel everyday selling drugs. Usually, drug dealers are very territorial over their established traps. We knowingly entered a trap that already had established drug dealers. I guess it was by the grace of a greater power that competing drug dealers did not bother us. We didn't even have a gun for protection! We were young kids that put ourselves in a very precarious situation.

Glenwood Rd.

Signs

My sister-from-another-mother once asked me, "How can you discern when God is talking to you?" My answer was, "You have to sit still, pay attention, and make sure you are mentally,

33

physically, and spiritually open to receive the message." I specifically call this my inner voice. During my short stint as a drug dealer, the creator tried to talk to me and warned me to stop selling drugs on four different occasions before I was either killed or arrested. In each situation, I was obviously not paying attention.

Sign One

Sign number one was when my friend and I were in the hotel room with a client that we sold crack to at the Old English Inn. In the early '90s we referred to individuals that experimented with drugs as "Geek Monsters" or "Js," which is a one letter acronym for "junky." So, we were having a conversation with this geek monster, and she was telling us about her family and how she doesn't communicate with them anymore because of her drug habit. In the midst of the conversation, I received a page (we did not have cell phones back then) from my girlfriend's brother indicating that we needed to meet him on the frontage road in front of the hotel. As soon as we stepped off the property and walked five minutes down the street, a slew of police cars swarmed on the hotel property and raided all the rooms. If not for the page, we would have been arrested in the raid. This close call with incarceration did not dissuade me from selling drugs, however.

Sign Two

Even though we sold drugs, we also had summer jobs. Sign number two came when a friend of mine and myself were on our way to pick up my partner in crime from work. My friend had a summer job in Scottdale, Georgia. So, of course we were utilizing the blue pinto to pick him up from work. Now I need you to understand that we were all either fifteen or sixteen, no one had a driver's license, the car was not registered, had no insurance, and we were "riding dirty" with crack and weed in the car. We were breaking a plethora of laws, to say the least.

Church Street.

As we were approaching the exit of Church Street in Decatur, the car stalled out and would not start. While we were sitting in the stalled pinto, a Turner County Police CSI (Crime Scene Investigation) Van pulled up directly beside us. We almost soiled our pants and had no idea what to do. Should we run? Should we stay? As the van pulled up beside us, the driver window rolled down and this white, pudgy female with blond hair pleasantly asked, "Do you guys need any help?" We quickly and calmly said, "No, we're fine," and she drove off. You would think that we would retire from selling drugs at that moment. I guess we were not that intelligent! Instead, we tried to start the car once more. It started right away, and we proceeded to pick up my friend from work.

Sign Three

Once we picked up my childhood friend from work in our old, very loud pinto, we proceeded to our next destination. As we were driving the car, we noticed that it stopped making noise. We were thinking that the car had suddenly started operating better without being fixed. Unbeknownst to us, the engine had locked up because the car ran out of oil. You would think that we would have stopped our illegal activities at this point, however we did not.

Sign Four

Every summer my family took a summer vacation. The summer of 1992 was no different. Before I left town I had to leave the drug stash with my partner in crime. We kept our drugs in a small leather pouch. I explained to my homeboy that I was going to leave the pouch in the mailbox for him to retrieve, which I did.

When I returned from my summer vacation, I did not think to check the mailbox because I knew that my friend had retrieved the package. This is an example of what happens when you make assumptions in life. Ultimately, my father checked the mailbox. Not only did he find mail, he also found a black leather pouch. My partner in crime failed to come by and pick up the package. Most parents would have looked in the pouch to see what it was. My father is not that type of person. He always gives an individual the benefit of the doubt. He simply brought the pouch to me and said,

"Is this yours?" he asked me as he handed me the pouch.

"Yes," I answered as I took it.

Now, you would think after four signs, clearly telling me to stop what I was doing, I would stop. Guess what! You are wrong!

Thirteen Bags of Crack, Three Bags of Weed

My drug career came to a screeching halt one fine summer morning in 1992. The previous night, I put the pouch of drugs in my book bag and then put the bag under some clothes in the bottom of my closet. That morning I woke up and my mother was standing over me holding the pouch of drugs in her hand. She had a look on her face that I would never forget. It was not a look of anger, but more of a look of disappointment. As she was questioning me about the drugs, she started crying. I would have preferred a beating over seeing her shedding tears. To this day, disappointing my mother is still the worst feeling I have ever experienced. Ultimately, I underwent drug-testing and had to attend counseling sessions with a family psychiatrist. That was the end of my career as a drug dealer. I lost my parents' trust and risked my freedom; yet, my delinquent behavior did not end there.

TANO

BUCKING THE SYSTEM

During my teenage years my delinquent behavior seemed to be unlimited. I did it all! I experimented with drugs and alcohol, attended adult clubs, and sold illegal narcotics. I ran away from home twice, snuck out of the house religiously, stole my parents' car, skipped school, and I was in a physical altercation with two assistant principals.

Running Away from Home

The first time I ran away from home was on my fifteenth birthday. How asinine was that? I planned on celebrating my birthday with my neighborhood friends at Sharon's Showcase. However, my parents had different plans. My mother informed me that I was too young to go to the club and I had to stay home that night. I became infuriated and I stormed out of the house and ran away so that I could go to the club. I stayed with a childhood friend and returned home forty-eight hours later to two very unenthused parents.

The second time I ran away was when a friend of mine left a voicemail on my pager stating that he was in jail and needed to be bailed out. As a result, I blindly solicited funds from our classmates in a campaign to spring him out of jail. My father told me I could not go, but I tried anyway. When I tried to leave, my father jacked me up and I found out the difference between man strength and little boy strength. "Bobby don't hurt him!" my mother screamed as my father grabbed me. My father gave her the "I got this" look and she backed down. Ultimately, I left anyway. Later that night, I found out that my friend played a cruel joke on me and he was actually never arrested. Through this experience, I started realizing that my parents were my *real friends*, not my so call homeboys from the "hood."

Sneaking Out of the House

I am not quite sure why I used to sneak out of the house. It wasn't like I did anything different at night than what I did during the day. I think back to how extremely bold I was as an adolescent, as well as how extremely dumb I was. My usual routine was to wait until my parents were asleep and climb out of my window. Sometimes my childhood friend Eric would steal his mother's car and pick me up at the corner of my street and we would visit one of our female acquaintances. Of course, the girls lived with their parents, so we usually sat at the end of their driveway and talked, nothing too earth shattering. I guess sneaking out of the house gave me some type of bizarre thrill. Perhaps it was the same feeling of excitement I got from stealing my parents' car.

DELINQUENT TO DOCTOR

Stealing the Car

My mother taught me how to drive a stick shift car at the age of fourteen. Consequently, I had the ability to drive twenty-four months before I was legally able to drive. On one hand, it was great that I was ambitious and had the willingness to acquire the skill of driving before my time. On the other hand, learning to drive at an early age further fueled my delinquent behavior. As a result, I started taking my parents car without their permission at fourteen.

I only took the car at certain times. I learned early on that my parents were very routine and predictable. I noticed that whenever they went out, they would always come home by a certain time. The time they came home was contingent on their activity, which might be attending an athletic competition or some type of social gathering with their friends. For example, if they went to a Super Bowl Party, it was almost a given that they would be home within an hour after the event was over. Whenever I knew they were going to an event, I made sure that I took one of my parents' sets of keys and put them away, because I knew they were going together in one car and only needed one set of keys. Therefore, I knew they would not be looking for the other set.

Usually, when I stole the car I would just drive around or visit one of my female friends. I made sure that when I brought the car back that I put it back the way it was. I made sure that I put the seats back how my parents had them adjusted. I paid attention to

40

how the radio station was set, as well as the volume level. I had to put all the mirrors and seats back to my parents' desired position. All these adjustments required special attention, because I find that most people treat their cars like a pair of shoes, specialized to fit them. Therefore, if the seat was too far back, the mirrors moved, the radio was changed from a jazz to hip-hop or rap station, or the volume was too high, it would have been obvious that I had been in the car.

I thought I had pretty much perfected the art of stealing my parents' car. Historically, all individuals that "do dirt" commit one fundamental mistake, which is thinking that they will never get caught. Anyone that continuously does dirt eventually either gets caught or experiences a slip-up. In my case it was the latter.

It was October of 1992. I remember the month and the year, because the Atlanta Braves were playing the Toronto Blue Jays in the World Series and I remember time went back an hour because of Daylight Savings Time. My best friend at the time was a young lady named Kia. This night, my parents had plans to attend a World Series party. So, of course I started preparing for my "joy ride." I asked a few questions pertaining to where they were going and what time they were leaving. I purposely did not ask too many questions because I did not want to draw suspicion. I proceeded to hide the keys and called my partner-in-crime, Kia, to see what the plan was for the night.

41

Whenever I took the car I knew I was wrong and I often thought about the ramifications if I was ever caught by my parents or the authorities. I think at this point in my life I was just bold, stupid, and did not care. I've heard some older people refer to this state of mind as being, "Young, dumb, and full of cum." In retrospect, I have to concur. With that being said, Kia and I decided that we would have a low key evening. We decided to pick up our respective companions, Craig and Tamara, and go back to my house to watch the World Series. We all lived in close proximity to each other, so it took no time to pick everyone up.

Once we returned to my house, we played cards, watched the game, and just kicked it. Now, remember what I said earlier about my parents being routine and predictable. I think we were having so much fun, that time slipped away from us. We looked up and the baseball game was over. Everybody was like, "Oh shit! We have to go!" I had to get everyone home, get back to my house, and put the car back exactly how it was before I took it. Let me also add that my vision was not very good at night and I did not like wearing my glasses.

Everyone moved swiftly to put the house back in order and I proceeded to drop everyone off at home. I dropped Craig off first, Tamara next, and I was dropping Kia off last. Everything was going great until we got to Covington Highway, which is a major street in Decatur.

So, we were driving down Covington Highway, speeding, trying to get Kia home. As we were coming down Covington Highway, I had to make a quick left turn at a four-way intersection. With a combination of speeding, night blindness (I wasn't wearing my glasses), and stupidity, I missed the turn and attempted to make it anyway. Instead of completing the left turn successfully, we jumped the curb and landed in very thick brush, about eight feet down, in a ditch. We were mortified! I think we both thought we were dead for a moment.

Once we realized we were not dead or injured, we had to figure out how to get the car out of the ditch before someone called the police. We would have definitely been arrested for violating various laws. First, I tried to put the car in reverse and just back out of the ditch, but I was unsuccessful. The only thing I accomplished was partly burning out the clutch, because the car had no traction. Throughout this process, Kia was trying to calm me down, because I was freaking out!

Kia tells me that everything is going to be alright. I've read stories about people developing incredible strength and increasing levels of adrenaline in life or death situations, like a mother lifting a car off their child with one hand, but I had never experienced this phenomenon personally. I became a believer this particular night. Kia tells me that she is going to get out and push the car while I drive in reverse. She gets out and pushes the car from the passenger side door with her right hand and shoulder, I threw the car in reverse, and we were out of the ditch within seconds. All we could say was "Thank you GOD"! I dropped Kia off safely and went back home before my parents returned.

Once I got home, I did a complete inspection of the car, praying there were no major damages. The only external damages I found were a few inconspicuous scratches, which were only noticeable if you looked at the car closely. However, the clutch was slightly worn, which caused a slight stench when operating the car. Next, I went in the house, hoped for the best and went to sleep. The next morning, Kia came over to hang out. My mother drove the car to church and when she returned, she mentioned that the car had a funny smell. Kia and I looked at each other and we had a look on our face that basically said, "If you only knew." Needless to say, I never stole my parents' car again.

Skipping School

As an adult, I understand that a good education is vital to levels of success or lack of success in life. When I was younger I did not quite grasp that concept. During my high school years, my life was a complete paradox. Although I displayed high levels of delinquent behavior and associated with other young brothers that displayed high levels of delinquent behavior, I was in all advance classes. I made relatively good grades, but I could have done much better. In retrospect, and knowing what I know now, I could have been valedictorian. Instead I chose to skip school and continue my delinquent behavior. Even though I did not mind skipping class or school, I was not completely stupid. I understood that I had a father and mother that were still holding me accountable to certain areas in my life, including academics and school attendance.

I liked skipping school, but I had to be smart about it, if that makes sense. My version of intelligently skipping school was to only skip when teachers usually didn't require any important assignments to be turned in or give any quizzes or tests. Those days were Mondays and Fridays during the spring quarter and the days before and after holidays.

My logic was very flawed. I was never caught for committing truancy (the legal term for skipping school). I now understand that drinking alcohol, smoking marijuana, and the early sexual activity that I engaged in while skipping school could have been satisfied after school or on the weekends. Honestly, I should not have been engaged in those activities in the first place. Yet, these forms of negative self-discovery pales in comparison to what I did next.

Fighting the Principal

In the spring of 1993, I was really "smelling myself." During my sophomore year I was one of six sophomores to start on the varsity football team, I had plenty of money in my pocket from working at the local mall, and various females had a romantic interest in me. I believed I was invincible and I had a very bad attitude. When my parents discuss this period of my life, they describe that I left home one day and when I came back, they did not recognize who I was. During this time, I had a job at Baker's

Shoes, in South DeKalb Mall in Decatur. Football and wrestling season was over, therefore I was not involved in any extracurricular activities, and had a pocket full of money and idle time on my hands.

Along with smoking, drinking, and being truant, I was also constantly fighting and having confrontations with teachers and principals. I was suspended about four times consecutively. The assistant principal, Mr. Jones, warned me, "If I see you in my office one more time, you will be expelled." This encounter with Mr. Jones really resonated with me. I did not want to be expelled from Turner County Schools, so I was trying to be on my best behavior. However, that came to a screeching halt in April of 1993.

I was coming from lunch and I spotted my girlfriend, Sheila, walking down the hallway with her best friend. I noticed this guy named James walk up behind her and put his arm around her shoulder. As I'm watching this ordeal unfold, I'm playing out various scenarios in my head. Presently, I called this technique, "Playing the Movie Out." Playing the movie out is a concept that I developed, where I play out various scenarios in certain situations and weigh out the various outcomes. I attempted to choose the most optimal outcomes, but it did not always turn out for the best.

I knew if I had a physical altercation with James, that I would be expelled and I *definitely* didn't want that to happen! Even though I played the movie out, I still made the wrong choice. I saw James' arm around Sheila's shoulder and I reacted prematurely. I extended my arm, I made my hand into a fist, and I walked directly towards James and put my fist in his chest. In my mind that was not a punch, I merely just pushed him away from my girlfriend. I believed I was justified, but I've also learned in life that even though you can justify why you do something, it doesn't necessarily make it right. As a result of my actions, James slightly slapped me. I say he slightly slapped me because there wasn't very much force behind the slap. He barely touched me. At this point I had to have a conversation with myself. I said, "Self, if I knock this boy out, Mr. Jones is going to expel me." Therefore, I reframed from retaliating and I walked away. Nevertheless, I was still summoned to Mr. Jones' office.

At first, I was like, "Here we go again," but my second thought was, "I didn't fight so I should be cool." Yeah right! Boy did he destroy my delusions of grandeur! Once I entered the office, I was facing Mr. Jones and James. Mr. Jones instructed James and I to explain our versions of the altercation in the hallway. I was calm, cool, and collected, until Mr. Jones informed us that we were both going to be suspended three days for fighting - pending a hearing. At that point, Mr. Jones' words started ringing in my head, "If I see you in my office again, you will be expelled." I think I had an out of the body experience, because I lost my mind!

I became extremely belligerent and yelled, "If I knew I was going to get suspended, I would have knocked his ass out!" Mr. Jones' office was not very big. James and I were standing next to each other in front of his desk and he was sitting down facing us. I proceeded to go around Mr. Jones to use the phone, without permission. I picked up the phone and he snatched the phone out of my hand and proceeded to hang the phone up. I snatched the phone right back and said, "I'm calling my daddy!" Now we are in a full fledge verbal altercation, going at it. He proceeds to call the other assistant principal, Dr. Lewis into the office, apparently to calm me down, however it was too late. I said, "Fuck this, I'm out!" and proceeded to leave the office. Dr. Lewis attempted to impede my progress and I allegedly slammed his arm in the door before I fled the office. I say allegedly, because I don't feel I slammed his arm in the door. Nevertheless, you know there are three sides to every story: My side, your side, and the truth.

Once I left school grounds, I went over my friend Jason's house to call my father. At that time, my father was enlisted in the United States National Guard. I told my father my side of the story and he instructed me to meet him at the school. Once I returned to the school, campus security and administrators were awaiting my arrival. Shortly after, my father arrived in his military uniform visibly upset and wanted to know the whole story.

Mr. Jones proceeded to present his side of the story and I became upset again, because I believed he was embellishing various aspects of the altercation. He stated that I pushed him and I slammed Dr. Lewis' arm in the door as I was leaving the office. As he was giving his side of the story, I kept interrupting him out of frustration. I believed he was spinning the story to suit his agenda. I knew he wanted to expel me from Avery High School and the entire Turner County School System. When it was my father's time to speak, he simply stated that although he believed that I was in the wrong, he also believed that Mr. Jones could have handled the situation better. He went on to say that he shouldn't have come down to my level and that he handled the current situation, as well as my previous indiscretions, more like a child.

Needless to say, I was suspended for a minimum of ten days, pending a hearing before the Student Evidentiary Hearing Committee. The Student Evidentiary Hearing Committee is a committee of certified personnel, authorized by the Turner County Board of Education who hears student discipline cases. Once they hear a student's case, they determine whether to expel or suspend them.

I was charged with repeated violations, fighting with another student, and having a physical altercation with two assistant principals. During the hearing, James and my girlfriend were called in to testify. Mr. Jones gave his side and I finally gave my side. Additionally, the individuals overseeing the hearing examined my academic and behavior file, and read letters that were provided by teachers in my favor. Even though my behavior file was atrocious, my academic file was exceptional, and the teachers' letters were very positive. The committee members seemed to be in a bit of a quandary. My guess is that they were trying to figure out how a young man that has earned good grades in advance classes display such deplorable behavior. I presumed from my punishment that the committee believed that even though they had to punish me, they did not want to make it *too* severe because I had the potential to do much better in school.

Ultimately, I was expelled from all Turner County Schools and sentenced to one quarter at the Turner County Alternative School located in Scottdale for supposedly assaulting two assistant principals. Now, if the committee members really believed that I committed this atrocity I feel that my sentence would have been lengthier than one quarter. Expulsion meant that I could not participate in any Turner County School System activities or be on any of its properties. Since this episode took place early spring quarter, I was suspended for the remainder of the quarter and expelled for the fall quarter. Luckily, all my teachers agreed to allow me to complete my assignments at home and my parents delivered them to the school. I completed my sophomore year and qualified to advance to the 11th grade. My next stop was the Turner County Alternative School.

Alternative School

The summer was over and it was time for me to start my sentence. In 1993, the Turner County Alternative School was referred to as Hamilton. I remember my father telling me that I needed to use this moment in life as a time of reflection and start making better decisions. There were no school buses that transferred students to Hamilton, so my mode of transportation was either my parents dropping me off or taking MARTA. You do not know what you're missing until it is gone. No more "free limo" (big yellow buses) rides to and from school.

Hamilton was a school designated for individuals that could not function in a mainstream school setting. Students were sent there for committing such indiscretions as burglary, bringing weapons to school, possession of illegal substances, repeated fighting violations, and destruction of school property, just to name a few. Just like prison, the function of this school was intended to rehabilitate students in order for them to return to their home school. Unfortunately, some students were rehabilitated and others individuals came out worse than when they attended their home schools (just like prison).

The school was set up to instill discipline and structure. The classrooms were small and they had a zero tolerance policy to combat discipline problems. Zero tolerance means they already made you aware of the rules, therefore if you broke the rules at Hamilton; the immediate consequence was expulsion from alternative school. This school even had jail cells at the end of the hallway for students who committed certain offenses. More serious infractions earned you a ride to jail. You were then expelled from alternative school and you had to serve your sentence at home or find another county that would take you. If you missed any days of school, you had to continue where you left off when you returned.

Therefore, if you were expelled from the county and the alternative school for a year, you were a year behind in your educational career.

With such strict rules, most of us adhered to the rules and at least pretended like we had conformed to our new - and hopefully temporary - environment. This was my new world for one quarter, which was roughly twelve weeks. As it turned out, it was one of the best things to happen to me, because it gave me time to reflect on my life. It made me really think about my future and what direction I wanted to go in, the positive progressive route or the negative non-progressive route. I chose the former. I completed Hamilton with a 3.7 grade point average (GPA) and a new outlook on life. The one major drawback was that Hamilton was not a traditional school. A major difference was that they only offered five classes per quarter compared to six classes in a regular public school. Therefore, in order for me to graduate on time I had to make up that class. Teachers and former students that attended Hamilton suggested that I attend Open Campus.

Open Campus

Open Campus was another alternative school. However, Open Campus was not necessarily for individuals with discipline problems. Different students had various reasons why they attended Open Campus. Generally, teenage mothers, recent juvenile parolees, and students who were held back for academic deficiencies but wanted to graduate on time with their class attended Open Campus. My reason for attending Open Campus was to make up the one class I missed. I decided to attend Open Campus, but not right away. I wanted to go back to my home school, for at least one quarter, because I missed my classmates. I returned to Avery High School for the second quarter and enrolled into Open Campus the following spring.

Open Campus had a unique set-up. The traditional public school year was divided into three quarters that were twelve weeks per quarter. Open Campus had six quarters that were six weeks per quarter. So you could satisfy twice as many credits in a shorter period of time. Open Campus also allowed students to govern themselves and had somewhat of a zero tolerance discipline policy. However, their zero tolerance was slightly different from Hamilton's zero tolerance policy. Sounds pretty good, right?

Open Campus classes were two hours instead of one. Each class was divided into two halves, giving students a break in between the first and second half of classes. We were allowed to miss a maximum of three days or six halves per class, per quarter. If we missed more than three days or six halves, we were automatically withdrawn from the class. If we came late to class, were a discipline problem, or caused any disruption during instructional time, the teacher had the authority to dismiss us from class and that would count as a half. We could eat in class, students would smoke outside in-between classes, and you could come and go as you pleased.

🔥 DELINQUENT TO DOCTOR

Unlike high school, there was no one on your case about what you should be doing, and where you should be. It was more like college. As with many tools in life, they can be used for good as well as evil. To drive this point home, I often use the example of water. Water is approximately 71% of the earth's surface and is the source of life for all plants, animals, and humanity. However, water can be deadly in certain situations - such as tsunamis and hurricanes. Open Campus was a great environment for self-motivated, driven, and mature individuals. I utilized my opportunity at Open Campus by making up for my lost credits. I even gained extra credits, which put me ahead of my peers. I was in a position to graduate earlier. It seems like I was headed in the right direction, but every time I took one step forward, it seemed like I took five steps back.

Cobb County

In the 1990s, Cobb County was a predominately Caucasian county in the Metro Atlanta area. If you were an individual of another ethnicity, especially African, it was guaranteed that if you drove through Cobb County, you would experience some form of racial profiling. Guaranteed! In 1994, I had a friend named Dexter who used to break into cars to steal radios and rims. It was called "creeping" back then. He even had a seemingly, full proof way of not being caught. He would only go creeping at night, during thunderstorms. The logic was that most people are fast asleep in the middle of the night, especially during a thunderstorm. He would also toss broken pieces of a spark plug at the car window to shatter it quietly. Once the window was shattered, it was easy to unlock the car and attain items from inside.

On August 12, 1994, three of my friends and I decided to take a "stupid pill," as my father would say. It was a very inclement night, and Calvin, Jason, Dexter, and I decided to go creeping. We decided to go to Cobb County. Yes, Cobb County! Why in the world would we want to go creeping in one of the most racist, if not the most racist county in metro Atlanta? Our justification was that communities in Cobb County would have cars with more upscale items to steal.

Later that night, we found ourselves driving through a thunderstorm, looking for the perfect target. We chose apartment complexes over communities with single family homes because they were easier to survey quickly. With what we were doing, time was of the essence. After driving through two or three complexes we found the area that we thought would be best for the pickings. To this day, we refer to this apartment complex as the apartment with the windmill, because it had a big windmill in front of the complex. When we got out of the car to look around, we all had this eerie feeling that something was not right, but we kept looking for easy targets to break into. This was another incident in my life that taught me to always listen to my inner voice. We finally decided to leave when we couldn't find a suitable car to break into. We should have decided to leave about five minutes earlier!

DELINQUENT TO DOCTOR

As we were leaving the complex, the Cobb County Police met us at the entrance. We turned onto the street and started to flee, but the police flashed his lights, turned around and stopped us in our tracks. We were all trying to get our story together to avoid being arrested. The police walked up to the car and asked us why we were in the neighborhood. We basically said we got lost and we were on our way back to the expressway. All of a sudden, one police officer turned into four police officers, and then fifteen police officers. Every officer was a Caucasian male and I remember them having German Shepherds.

The police officers were not buying our story about being lost. They took all of us out of the car, frisked us, and deliberately placed us in separate police cars to individually interrogate us. They were trying to get us to confess to breaking into cars. They even claimed that one of the residents taped us with their camcorder. We all pretty much said, "I don't know what you are talking about, we are simply lost." They also took pictures of us and they wanted to know our names and addresses. Since one of our rules was never to carry identification while creeping, I did not have my I.D. on me. When they asked for my name, I told them I was Raymond Middlebrooks (our recently deceased friend). I thought I was being clever by using a deceased person's identity. My rationale was that even if I get arrested, they will have my picture, but they will have a different name. My plans were foiled, because when they asked the other guys my name, they each gave my full government name. Mother sucker!!

While we were in the patrol cars, we could hear the communication going back and forth over the police patrol car radios. The police officers were running our information as well as the car's information. We kept hearing, "It doesn't match! It doesn't match!" It wasn't until they took us out of the cars that we understood what was going on. Apparently, there were individuals in the same complex, breaking into cars before we got there. That is why the authorities were called initially. This was a classic case of being in the wrong place at the wrong time. We were four young African males on a side street, at night, in Cobb County, in the rain, surrounded by approximately fifteen Caucasian police officers with German Shepherds. One of the police officers told us that the make of the car, and the license plate did not match with the make of the car and license plate they were actually looking for. However, he said, "I am going to flip this coin. Heads you go to jail and tails you don't." I was praying it was tails. When the coin landed, it was tails. I was so relieved but it didn't matter! The officer said, "You are going to jail anyway."

They put Calvin in a car by himself. The officers put two sets of handcuffs on me and crossed my arms. He connected Jason to my left side and Dexter to my right side and put all three of us in the back of a patrol car. If you have ever been in the back of a patrol car, you know it's uncomfortable with one person in the back, never mind three. It was horrible! As we were being transported to the Cobb County Jail, I kept thinking to myself, "How in the world am I going to explain this to Bobby and Carolyn Rosemond?"

Cobb County jail mug shot.

Once we arrived at the facility, we had to empty our pockets, remove our shoestrings and belts, and put them in a paper bag. Next, we were fingerprinted and we had to take mug shots. Since they could not charge us with breaking into cars, they had to find something creative to charge us with. Calvin's car was an old mustang that always had some type of mechanical malfunction, so he kept a toolbox in the trunk. Since there was a toolbox in the trunk, we were all charged with possession of tools, with the intent to commit a crime. We did not commit a crime, but they charged us because we *could* have committed a crime. We were also

charged with loitering, and I was charged with giving a false name

for trying to use Raymond's name.

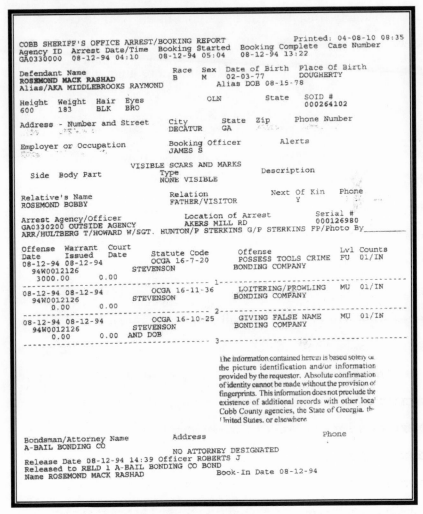

```
COBB SHERIFF'S OFFICE ARREST/BOOKING REPORT           Printed: 04-08-10 08:35
Agency ID   Arrest Date/Time   Booking Started  Booking Complete  Case Number
GA0330000   08-12-94 04:10     08-12-94 05:04   08-12-94 13:22

Defendant Name                     Race  Sex  Date of Birth  Place Of Birth
ROSEMOND MACK RASHAD                B     M    02-03-77       DOUGHERTY
Alias/AKA MIDDLEBROOKS RAYMOND                 Alias DOB 08-15-78

Height  Weight  Hair  Eyes              OLN          State    SOID #
600     183     BLK   BRO                                     000264102

Address - Number and Street        City     State  Zip   Phone Number
                                   DECATUR   GA

Employer or Occupation             Booking Officer      Alerts
                                   JAMES S

                      VISIBLE SCARS AND MARKS
    Side  Body Part       Type              Description
                          NONE VISIBLE

Relative's Name                    Relation             Next Of Kin  Phone
ROSEMOND BOBBY                     FATHER/VISITOR        Y

Arrest Agency/Officer              Location of Arrest        Serial #
GA0330200 OUTSIDE AGENCY              AKERS MILL RD          000126980
ARR/HULTBERG T/HOWARD W/SGT. HUNTON/P STERKINS G/P STERKINS FP/Photo By

Offense   Warrant  Court
Date      Issued   Date    Statute Code      Offense            Lvl Counts
08-12-94 08-12-94          OCGA 16-7-20       POSSESS TOOLS CRIME FU 01/IN
 94W0012126              STEVENSON            BONDING COMPANY
   3000.00     0.00
---------------------------------- 1 ------------------------------------
08-12-94 08-12-94          OCGA 16-11-36      LOITERING/PROWLING  MU 01/IN
 94W0012126              STEVENSON            BONDING COMPANY
    0.00       0.00
---------------------------------- 2 ------------------------------------
08-12-94 08-12-94          OCGA 16-10-25      GIVING FALSE NAME   MU 01/IN
 94W0012126              STEVENSON            BONDING COMPANY
    0.00       0.00 AND DOB
---------------------------------- 3 ------------------------------------
                                   The information contained herein is based solely on
                                   the picture identification and/or information
                                   provided by the requestor. Absolute confirmation
                                   of identity cannot be made without the provision of
                                   fingerprints. This information does not preclude the
                                   existence of additional records with other local
                                   Cobb County agencies, the State of Georgia, the
                                   United States, or elsewhere

Bondsman/Attorney Name       Address                      Phone
A-BAIL BONDING CO
                             NO ATTORNEY DESIGNATED
Release Date 08-12-94 14:39 Officer ROBERTS J
Released to RELD 1 A-BAIL BONDING CO BOND
Name ROSEMOND MACK RASHAD              Book-In Date 08-12-94
```

The arrest report.

After we were processed into the system, we were given a

chance to make one phone call and they placed us in a holding cell.

The cell was about 16x20 feet in size, with two long parallel benches. There was a five-foot wall towards the back of the cell, with a toilet behind it. At any given time that night, there were approximately fifteen to twenty people in the holding cell. Men in there were arrested for selling drugs, fleeing the police, assault, domestic violence, and probation violation, among other various violations.

It was a very funny, scary, and an eye-opening experience. We were in the holding cell for about nine hours, and were informed that if we did not make bail by a certain time, we would be placed in the general population. We were all praying we did not have to experience that. My father bailed me out right before they were going to put me in population. Unfortunately, the other guys' parents did not come in time and they went to general population, but only for a small amount of time. That was a long ride home. Needless to say, I never went creeping again. I came out of alternative school unscathed, trying to finish my senior year on a positive note. However, it was not looking good for the home team. Like I said previously, every time I took one step forward, I took five steps back.

Graduation

After a tumultuous summer, I returned to my home school for the purpose of playing football my senior year. I started varsity football my sophomore year, missed my junior year because I was a knucklehead, and believed I had some unfinished business to take care of. I had a pretty good year and I was satisfied with my performance and my last experience as a football player on the high school level. I never had fantasies of playing football on the collegiate or professional level. At this point in my life, I was just trying to figure out what my next step was going to be. Ultimately, I decided to return to Open Campus and graduate from high school early. My high school career was complete on March 10, 1995 - three months before my classmates were finished. Then I decided to have a graduation party to celebrate.

Varsity Football Team, 1995.

Party King

Among other things, I was known for throwing amazing parties. As I was closing out my adolescent years, two classmates, Robert, and Richard approached me about throwing a party with them. I replied, "Sure, why not." I had been throwing successful parties at different venues in Metro Atlanta since age sixteen.

My sixteenth birthday party flyer.

I created a very simple formula. First, I always understood male to female ratios. I understood that there should be more females than males whenever there was a party, because when males become bored, they do stupid things, like fight each other. If there are a high number of females at the party, the guys would be entertained.

The pool party flyer.

Also, we only gave flyers to females, because we knew if females were talking about going to a party, the males would automatically show up. We also featured a "booty shaking" dance contest and we gave away a cash prize. Contests had various names such as "Rump Shaker," "Wet Cat," and "Fat Cat." Finally,

I let all females in for free until a certain time. This guaranteed that the females would be happy, because they didn't have to pay, and the males were happy, because it was plenty of females. I was always happy because I made plenty of money, and the party was off the chain.

A party just because.

In preparation for the party we passed out flyers to schools all over the Metro Atlanta Area. The weather on the day of the party was perfect. We paid for the venue, D.J., food, and drinks. We arranged for girls to frisk guys and guys to frisk girls, to prevent weapons from entering the venue. The only thing that we had to do was be great hosts for our guests. The party started at 8:00 p.m. and it was crunk (the party was jumping) by 9:15 p.m.

Graduation party.

As planned, the male to female ratio was perfect. There were no fights and everyone had a great time, and yes we did have the "Fat Cat" contest, but only one young lady participated. She had such a great performance, no one really cared that she was the only one stripping. We were obliged to give her the $50 prize.

65

Ultimately, the police came and shut the party down because there were too many cars and teenagers in one place. They had a helicopter, roadblocks, and patrol cars everywhere. It was pandemonium! I recall one police officer wondering out loud, "Did Freaknik start early this year?" Needless to say, the party was a success.

SITA

THE PARTY IS OVER

The next morning after the graduation party, I awoke to realize that the party was over, figuratively, and literally. Not only was my graduation party over, but my childhood was also over. Up until this point, all my goals were set for me. The main goals were advancing from one grade to the next. Since I just recently finished my required years of education, it was time to figure out my next move. I used to tell my students, "When you graduate from high school you have to find a way to buy your own toothpaste, soap, and underwear. At that point, your parents are no longer required to take care of you."

What am I Going To Do?

I found myself in the position of a high school graduate with no projected goals. However, I knew I had to do something, because I did not want to end up as the old dude still living with his parents. I really had no idea what I wanted to do with my life. At that time I was hanging out with this brother named Omar, because both of my closest friends were booed up (in relationships). Omar was about to graduate from a neighboring high school and was planning to enlist into the U.S. Army. He suggested that I join the military as well.

ARMY

In the words of Furious Styles from *Boyz N the Hood*, "Don't ever go in the Army Tre, Black man ain't got no place in the Army." I agreed with Furious, but at the time, I believed my options were very limited. I was desperate. Omar explained to me that we could enter the military on the buddy plan. The buddy plan allowed new recruits to experience basic training, technical school, and the first duty station together.

The Army started looking pretty good to me. So, I started the process of joining the military. I took the required test, which was the ASVAB and received a high score. ASVAB is an acronym for Armed Services Vocational Aptitude Battery (ASVAB). It is a timed multi-aptitude test, which is given at over 14,000 schools and Military Entrance Processing Stations (MEPS) nationwide and is developed and maintained by the Department of Defense. After the test, I filled out all the paperwork. The next step was for the recruiter to do a criminal background check. Uh Oh! Red Flag! Remember that little incident that took place about a year prior in Cobb County? It came back to bite me in the butt.

Apparently, the U.S. Army was not keen on allowing individuals into the military with open court dates. Ultimately, I did not go to the military. Nor had I heard from the Cobb County Authorities since my father picked me up from jail. My father and

I contacted them instead. Within a couple of weeks, we were given a court date and the case was eventually dismissed because of insufficient evidence. I was now back at square one - What am I going to do with my life? As it turned out, being arrested a year earlier was a blessing in disguise. Shortly after, I received a letter from Benedict College, a nearby Historically Black College (HBCU) in South Carolina.

South Carolina is Not That Bad

The letter stated that Benedict College was trying to establish a football team after not having one for thirty years. The recruiters were trying to staff their inaugural team after three decades. As I read the letter, I questioned my next move. My father and I discussed my options, which were limited, and decided at the very least, we should visit the campus. My father suggested that if I did not like it I could always go to the Air Force as a second option. So, we journeyed to Columbia to visit the campus.

The ride to Columbia was approximately three hours which was far enough to get away from home to start my independence, but close enough to get home quickly, if needed. Once we arrived on campus, I was very intrigued by the dormitories, bookstore, cafeteria, and the yard. The possibility of attending this school was exciting! We also ventured into the city of Columbia. Right across the street was Allen University, another HBCU. The University of South Carolina was down the street, and South Carolina State and Clafflin College, two other HBCUs, were less than forty-five minutes away in Orangeburg, South Carolina. There were also four major malls in the area, and a large population of Black people. My overall response was, "Well it's not Atlanta, but I think I can handle it." I returned home to start preparing myself for my first year at Benedict College.

Benedict College campus.

SABA

THE COLLEGE YEARS

When I came home I discussed my collegiate plans with two high school friends, Walter and Xavier. From the information I shared with them, they were also interested in enrolling into school. I thought it was a great idea. We could all share the college experience together. In July of 1995, we officially started our college career at Benedict College. Initially, I was drawn to Benedict for the purpose of playing football, but I never played. Once I discovered that no scholarships were being offered for the first year, I decided to officially end my football career and concentrate on my academics full-time. Shortly, Walter and Xavier followed suit and quit the team.

First Semester

My first semester of school was life changing. This was my first taste of living away from home. I officially had to fend for myself. The first semester was fun, but challenging at the same time. I was originally assigned a roommate who I was not familiar with. However, I finagled a roommate change to have Walter as my roommate. Xavier was only about three rooms down the hall on the same floor. Everything about college was looking promising.

We were like newborn babies experiencing life for the first time. We had to figure out the proper way to fill out financial aid papers, choose a major, set up a class schedule, and find somewhere to buy hygiene products and a place to wash our clothes. Luckily, both Walter and Xavier were barbers, so getting our haircut was one less thing we had to worry about. However, one major challenge we were faced with was our introduction to pre-approved credit cards.

Credit Cards

The first time I received information about a credit card, I was intrigued as well as apprehensive. On one hand, I was excited about the idea of being able to buy things and pay for them later. At the same time, my father always taught me, that if something sounds too good to be true, it usually is. For the longest time, I could not figure out what the underlined catch was to credit cards, until I read the fine print on back of the credit card statement.

The first couple of sentences explained that one could make purchases and pay a minimum amount per month. Minimum payments were as low as $7 per month. Apparently, most of my peers only read the first two lines. I decided to read further. Subsequent lines illustrated that interest would accrue at the end of each 30-day billing cycle if there was a balance. My father's advice proved to be accurate. I decided to accept my pre-approved credit card, but I did not use it until I gained employment at a local shoe store at Columbia Mall.

Since I previously had retail experience at Jarman's Shoes back home, I was able gain employment fairly easy at Jarman's Shoes in Columbia Mall. Shortly after, Walter started working at JC Penny's, in the customer service section, and Xavier started working at Auntie's Ann Pretzels. You would think that with us being a little older, attending college, and gainfully employed that our days of delinquency were over, but they weren't. Walter worked in the customer service section of JC Penny's, and he had access to customers' credit card numbers.

Identity Fraud

One day, Walter decided to write a couple of the credit card numbers down on a piece of paper and bring it back to the dorm. Once he came home and shared with us what he had done, we decided to see if the numbers really worked. We used the numbers to order pizzas, sodas, hot wings and breadsticks from Dominoes. I bet you are wondering how we used credit card numbers without producing the credit card and valid identification. In 1995, certain establishments did not scrutinize credit card payments as closely as they do today.

I must say, we had a good thing going. We would order and pay for the pizzas by phone, and have our items delivered to the front of the campus. Each time a different person would go down and retrieve the order and sign the receipt with names like John

Wayne, Bill Clinton, or James Bond. We did this just about every night for a few weeks, but as the saying goes, "All good things must come to an end." Apparently, Dominoes started receiving notices that credit card numbers had been used erroneously at Benedict College. The company refused to deliver to our campus immediately. After successfully committing identity fraud in our first semester of college, we then decided to monopolize the marijuana market on campus.

Three Blunt Dimes

With us coming from Atlanta, the marijuana market was drastically different in Columbia. In Columbia a dime bag rendered a blunt and a half maybe two, and a nickel bag rendered one skimpy blunt. In Atlanta a dime ($10) bag rendered three blunts and a nickel ($5) bag gave you at least a blunt and a half. Xavier, Walter, and I were sitting around smoking one day and we had an epiphany. If we purchased a large quantity of weed and bagged up nickels and dimes according to Atlanta standards, we could make a killing.

We decided to buy a quarter pound of weed for three hundred dollars, we each contributed $100 a piece. We had three blunt dimes and 1 ½ blunt nickel bags. We did exactly what we had intended to do. However, one variable we did not expect was competition and haters (envy). Once we entered the market, all the individuals that had a weed habit abandoned their weed provider and came to us. As you can imagine, the guys that were selling weed before us were not happy and they let it be known by confronting us. We stood our ground and basically told them to get over it. Still, we feared they may possibly snitch on us. We ultimately decided that being the weed men on campus and possibly getting arrested was not worth risking our future. We sold the rest of the weed and ended our marijuana operation.

Exodus

Throughout all the nonsense, I still managed to complete the semester with a 3.2 GPA. Xavier and Walter also finished the semester with respectable GPAs. However, towards the end of the semester they informed me that they were leaving to return back home to Atlanta. Initially, I was devastated, because this was going to be the first time that I would have to function completely by myself. I was not used to being without my friends. I asked them why they were leaving. They simply said that Columbia was slow and boring, and they wanted to go back home. Xavier also explained that he needed to be home to raise his son.

Then There Was One

When I returned to school after the winter holiday, I found myself all alone in my dorm room. It was lonely at first, but I really enjoyed having my own room. Another welcomed change during the second semester of my freshman year is that my father allowed me to bring my car to school. Things were looking up. However, I experienced a small academic snag. That second semester I earned three Cs and two Ds. This was not my proudest

75

moment. My father told me if I did not get myself together, he was going to pull the plug on my college career and I would have to move back home.

I went home that summer and I did a lot of soul searching. This was the summer Atlanta was hosting the '96 Olympics, and there were people in town from all over the world. It was a very exciting time. Coming home after a year of living in a different environment, I found that I had evolved somewhat. My father used to always tell me stories about people he went to high school with and how some of them never left home and how they have the same conversations they had when they were in school. He explained that his classmates were stuck in 1965.

My experience was surreal, because I was experiencing this phenomenon only one year removed from high school. While, yes, I still engaged in drinking alcohol and smoking weed occasionally, those were not my only interests. In one year I experienced scheduling my own classes, college parties, and sorority girls. My old circle's conversations consisted of drinking, smoking, clubbing, and gossiping about former classmates. That experience showed me that when I went back to school, I had to start taking life more serious, or I would be back home reliving my glory years. I was not going to allow that to happen. I was motivated to get back to Columbia and continue my collegiate journey.

Moving Off-Campus

I decided to move off campus after returning from summer break. I've always been the type of person that made logic out of the decisions that I made. In order for me to move off campus, I had to convince my father that it would be beneficial for all parties involved, him and myself. Initially, I took the monetary approach. First, I examined the itemized cost of the tuition that my parents were presently paying. Next, I researched various properties and apartment complexes that I wanted to live in and the cost compared to what my parents were paying for me to live on campus.

Next, I showed my father the monthly expenses for living on campus compared to monthly expenses living off campus. I pointed out that living off campus was more cost effective than living in the dorms. Reluctantly, he agreed to me moving off campus. I was quite excited. Over the summer, I returned to Columbia to search for a house or apartment to rent. After searching apartment guides and homes for rent in the newspaper, I found a two-bedroom house in a part of town called "Forest Acres." Forest Acres was a quiet community in Columbia where a lot of retirees lived. The house I found was $375 per month, but since I had not established any credit, except for one Nation's Bank Discover credit card, my father agreed to be a co-signer on my rental agreement, which assisted me with building my credit. I finalized the one-year lease for the property and returned to Atlanta to prepare for my move.

Once I returned home, I started gathering items that I wanted for my new home. My mother even assisted me with putting a housewarming party together. My idea was to have a housewarming party in Atlanta consisting of my parents' friends, because I believed that they would bring better gifts than my friends. My assumption was correct. I received enough merchandise to furnish my entire house. When I returned to Columbia, I had my first official bachelor pad.

Everything was going great until I had somewhat of a mental breakdown. At the time, I did not know what was going on with me. In retrospect, I think I was just experiencing a feeling of uncertainty and for the first time in my life everything around me was unfamiliar. So, I called my father almost in tears and said I wanted to quit school and return home. Yes, I was punking out. He told me that he was not going to waste his money on tuition, if my heart was not into school and told me to come home. He said I could always go to the military. The next morning I woke up with great clarity.

Traffic Light Moment

I refer to this moment in my life as a "Traffic Light Moment." In western culture, many individuals say a light bulb went off whenever they had an extraordinary idea. I often wondered why people used the light bulb when they had a great idea or epiphany. The conclusion I came to was that because it was a great invention supposedly created by Thomas Edison with no mention of the contributions of Lewis Howard Latimer, a black inventor (I digress). Well, I do not relate to that example. I wanted an example that related to me; therefore I chose the traffic light, which was invented by Garrett Morgan. My traffic light moments allow me to stop to think about the issue at hand (red light). Next, evaluate and examine the issue with caution to engineer a plan of action (yellow light), and finally execute the plan (green light).

That morning of January 4, 1997, the murky waters of my life started to become very clear to me. I called my parents to thank them for all the times they disciplined and beat me for being out-of-pocket. I further said, "I deserved it, and it has helped me to become the man I am today." At that moment, I realized I was right where I needed to be and education was the key to my success. That was the very first time I started taking my education seriously. My path to consciousness had begun.

Up until that point, I had taken my education lightly and put forth a pretty mediocre effort. I studied half the time, sat in the back of the classroom, and did not take adequate notes in class. I remember being in my economic class one morning and my professor, Dr. Njoku, who was from Nigeria, was sharing some information with us that he said would prepare us for graduate school. I replied that if I graduated from college, I was never going back to school again and I started laughing. His reply was, "Don't be stupid, you are going to graduate school." It wasn't until my traffic light moment, did I truly understand what Dr. Njoku was attempting to do. He was trying to help us become extraordinary individuals.

Once I turned over a new leaf, I started studying more, sitting in the front of the classroom, taking better notes and taking my education more seriously. I went from earning low Bs and Cs, to mostly As and high Bs. You're probably thinking, "Wow! He finally got his life together." Well, not so fast. When I initially moved into my house, my father acted as an absent roommate by paying half of the rent each month. I believed it was my responsibly to find a roommate to relieve my father of this burden. Within seven months, I went through two roommates.

First Two Roommates

The first guy was cool, but his girlfriend was at the house everyday and I believed she talked too much, she was too loud, used too much toilet paper and my grandmother walked in on them having sex in the living room when her and my mother were visiting one weekend. It was quite annoying. Ultimately, that arrangement did not work out, because I told him I wanted one roommate not two, along with other grievances I had pertaining to his girlfriend.

He shared the conversation with his girlfriend and needless to say, she was not too happy. She took it upon herself to confront me and she ended up hitting me in the face. My first thought was to hit her back, but I thought about the consequences and refrained. I simply said, "I'm going to do like the white folks and call the police." She thought I was playing and stated she was not going anywhere. Once the police arrived, I stated that I wanted the young lady arrested for assaulting me. The police asked the girlfriend if she hit me. She responded, "Yes, but I didn't mean too." The police read her rights and she was off to jail. The roommate and I parted ways that day. I should have known something was wrong when the girlfriend inquired about the roommate vacancy and not him. A lesson learned.

My next roommate was my childhood friend Dexter from Atlanta. He enrolled into Benedict College after attending to some personal issues. After he settled his personal affairs, I welcomed him with open arms and it was all good for about three months, until additional personal issues in his life materialized. One morning he woke up and told me he was going to follow up on a job and he got in his car and drove home, leaving me to pay the rent by myself. Needless to say, I was highly pissed. Once again I found myself without a roommate, until one of my old dorm mates approached me with a solution to my ongoing dilemma.

My Jamaican Roommate

Shortly after Dexter left, I was on campus talking to one of my classmates about my roommate situation. He told me that he had the perfect roommate for me. I happily asked, "Great! Who is it?" He informed me that it was this Jamaican brother named

81

Shaka. I asked him, how he knew this guy. He stated he was the weed man. Initially, I thought it was a bad idea, and I was not interested in that arrangement. About two weeks later, I guess I had a lapse in judgment and I changed my mind.

I now found myself with a Jamaican roommate named Shaka who was trafficking thirty pounds of marijuana per week. I know! I know! - What was I thinking? This is what I was thinking. The arrangement Shaka and I had agreed upon was, I would allow him to live in my house, and he agreed to pay the entire rent, pay all the utilities, and pay for the groceries. He also agreed that if I brokered any deal to distribute any amount of marijuana, he would give me a percentage of the sale. Money was my motivation at this time in my life and I believed that this was a great situation for me.

The first week with Shaka as my roommate was great. All of a sudden Shaka's cousin Anthony shows up. Now I have two roommates, instead of one. I believe I let that situation slide because Shaka was taking care of all the bills. Another two weeks passed and another friend of Shaka's shows up. The friend was a short, portly guy with a gold grill in his mouth with fangs, and an S-curl in his hair, named Boss. Boss was a local hustler who committed various unlawful acts in the area. Before I knew it, I had three drug dealers living in my house.

So as I am entering into one of the most profound transitions of my life pertaining to my personal belief system, consciousness, and education, I found myself in a very precarious predicament.

On one hand, all my bills were being paid, I had extra money in my pocket from selling weed, and I was doing great in all my classes. On the other hand, my three roommates had strange people coming in and out the house, having unauthorized gatherings, and I started noticing patrol cars driving by the house periodically. I remember one time coming home and Shaka, Anthony, and Boss were attempting to open this large package in the kitchen. It was wrapped in layers of bubble wrap, cardboard, and cellophane surrounded by coffee grounds. Once they removed the wrappings, I discovered that what they were attempting to retrieve was thirty pounds of pure, uncut marijuana. It was so strong, that we had to open all the windows in the house, because we were getting a contact high from the fumes. This was the proverbial straw that broke the camel's back.

Once again, I had a traffic light moment as well as a moment of reflection. I was thinking to myself that I am in the process of matriculating through school on my way to graduating. The quandary that I found myself in was extremely dangerous, as well as stupid. I was jeopardizing my future in the name of money. If I was caught, I would go to jail, there would be no more college, and my father could possibly be implicated because his name was on the lease as a co-signer. At that moment I knew I had to get out of that situation as soon as possible.

DELINQUENT TO DOCTOR

The Escape

During this time in my college career, I was a first semester junior taking classes in my major. Through the classes I was attending in the business department, I met two brothers named Malcolm and Terrance. Malcolm and Terrance were from Sumter, South Carolina and they were roommates. Through our daily discussions we discovered that we had a lot in common. As we grew as classmates and friends, we shared various stories and experiences. I told them about my drug-dealing roommates. After sharing my story, Malcolm suggested that I could be roommates with him and Terrance. Ironically, their roommate was about to move out and they needed someone to take his place and my lease was due to expire at the end of the month. They invited me over that evening for me to check out the apartment and my potential bedroom, if I chose to take advantage of their offer. Needless to say, the apartment was great, the total rent would be $547 divided three ways, and the third room was the largest room. I was convinced, and ready to move in.

The creator was talking to me, and I was listening. This was definitely a situation where I had to discern that the creator was speaking to me. I found my escape and I did not hesitate. When I went home that evening, I informed my unwanted tenants that everyone had to be out of the house by the end of month, and that was the end of the conversation.

At the end the month, I moved out of my first bachelor's pad and moved in with my new roommates. The entire process went off without a hitch. About three weeks later, I heard through a third party that my former roommates were arrested for selling marijuana. This lesson taught me not to allow money to be my motivation. When you allow money to be your motivation, you will become a prostitute, figuratively speaking, and you will do anything to get it. I live by this philosophy today.

NANE

CONSCIOUSNESS

I must admit that I have not read the Bible in its entirety; however, there are certain passages that I have read that resonate with me today. One verse in particular is Corinthians I, chapter 13, verse 11 that states, "When I was a child, I talked like a child, I thought like a child, I reasoned like a child. When I became a man, I put childish ways behind me." When I moved in with Malcolm and Terrance, I was at a crossroads in my life - between childhood and manhood. Even though I had put many of my childish ways behind me, there was still some childish residue lingering. I was still a work in progress.

Up until that point, my roommate experience was horrendous. Becoming roommates with Malcolm and Terrance was truly a blessing. Not only did I escape from possible incarceration, but I also found two roommates that I got along with. All three of us were also in the school of business, with the exact same major. We were able to carpool together, study with each other, and share each other's textbooks. It was the perfect situation. Even though I escaped from my marijuana-selling roommates to a better situation, I had not quite let the weed go yet, I still smoked occasionally.

Let me clarify my weed smoking habit. I was not a habitual smoker, but more of a social smoker. I had never purchased a bag of weed, or even a blunt. Most of the guys I knew that smoked, usually smoked in settings where there were no females. That never made sense to me. I only smoked if there were females present. There was no concrete logic for this, just my logic.

Last Blunt

In the mid to late '90s, there was a popular music company/group known as *No Limit Records*, headed by CEO, Master P. At the time a *No Limit Soldier* concert ticket was the hottest ticket on the planet! In October of 1997, Master P and the No Limit Soldiers had a scheduled concert at the University of South Carolina Coliseum. I remember wanting to attend, but not having the finances to afford a ticket.

One Wednesday night I decided to attend a party at the Sheraton Hotel, which was sponsored by the local radio station. During the festivities, the radio station announced a contest. The prize was two tickets to the Master P concert. I really wanted to win those tickets. The contest consisted of one question. The question was, "What is Master P's real name?" At the time Master P was very popular, but unless you were a true fan, you did not know any personal information about him. It just so happens that I recently purchased and viewed Master P's first independent movie,

87

I'm Bout It, which was loosely based on his life. In the movie his name was Perry Miller. My assumption was that Perry Miller was his real name. So of course when I heard the question through the speakers, I ran to the DJ booth and answered with fervor, "Perry Miller." The DJ said, "You are correct!" and I won two tickets to see my favorite hip-hop act at that time. Later, I discovered my answer was incorrect. Master P's government name was Percy Miller not Perry Miller. Oh well, I still won the tickets. I guess the DJ did not do his due diligence to find the correct answer.

After winning the tickets, I had to decide who I was going to take. I asked myself who would like to go to this concert just as much as me. My choice was my homeboy Xavier back in Atlanta. I called to let him know if he could find a way to Columbia, he had a free ticket. He told me he would let me know if he could find a way to Columbia. During this time, I was hanging out with this young lady named Lisa that I met while working at Red Lobster. We had discussed the concert and also how Xavier would get there. During our conversation, one of her friends overheard us and inquired about my friend. Ultimately, I gave her Xavier's number and they started talking on the phone.

Fast forward to the day before the concert and Xavier still had not found a ride. On that same day I had been paging Lisa all day with no answer. When she finally called me back, I asked her if she was ok.

"Yes," she replied.

"Where are you?" I asked.

"Me and my friend are on our way to Atlanta to pick Xavier up and bring him back to Columbia for the concert," she responded.

"Wow, ok, I will see you when you get back!" I said with surprise.

Now, I don't know what Xavier said to the friend for her to drive all the way to Atlanta and pick him up, but he was on his way.

Once they arrived safely, we hung out for a while and went back to the apartment. The next day, both young ladies asked us to come over for a steak dinner. After we finished eating we went to the liquor store to buy a bottle of gin and we also went and purchased a dime bag of weed. We sat in my 1986 Volkswagen Golf and drank some gin and lime juice and smoked a partial blunt. We didn't finish the blunt because we did not want to be late for the concert. We arrived at the concert on time and we had a phenomenal time.

After the concert, we were supposed to meet the girls back at the friend's apartment. First, we decided to finish smoking the weed we purchased earlier. So, we found a side street and blazed it up. We finished the partial blunt and rolled up another one, and smoked that one as well. We were so high it was ridiculous! I couldn't feel my face! I was sitting in the car touching my face and I remember saying to myself, "I can't feel my face. Why can't I feel my face?" Then I thought, "Why in the world would I intentionally do this to myself?" It made absolutely no sense! Prior to this night, I smoked from time to time. However, on this night my traffic light moment informed me that my smoking days were over. The last time I smoked weed was after the Master P concert, in Columbia, South Carolina, October 13, 1997, continuously putting childish things behind me.

My Master P concert ticket stub.

3.0

In the process of me coming into my consciousness, my thirst for education escalated. Like in a game of chess, I started thinking of potential moves that I may want to make in the future. Graduate school was definitely a route that I wanted to eventually pursue. However, through my research I discovered that most graduate programs require a minimum GPA of 3.0. At that time, I think my cumulative GPA was 2.65. I went to my academic advisor for guidance on what I needed to do to increase my GPA to 3.0. I was informed that if I took a heavy load of classes and earned As and Bs, that I had a good chance to earn a 3.0. I told myself that I could do this.

That following semester was the second semester of my junior year and I decided to take nine classes, which equated to twenty-three credits. The minimum number of credits needed to qualify as a full-time student was sixteen credits. Everyone thought I was crazy and they also said that there was no way that I would be able to earn higher than a B in all nine classes. All the naysayers and their negative comments simply fueled my desire to be extraordinary.

Benedict College Commencement Ceremony, May 9, 1999.

I knew that taking nine classes would not be an easy feat, however I knew once I made it through the storm, I would be

91

stronger. I decided that I would not go to any parties, Freaknik, Bike Week, or to Daytona. I also decided not to consume any alcohol and not to cut my hair until the semester concluded. I had classes five days a week, from 8:00 a.m. to 10:00 p.m. for sixteen weeks. When I was not in class, I was either writing a paper or studying for a test or quiz. To make the situation even more interesting, I elected to write and defend my senior thesis a year earlier than required. This process was one of the greatest challenges in my life.

		Spring Semester 1997/1998			
ACC 232	PRIN OF ACCT II	A	3.00	12.0
ACC 333	MANAGERIAL ACCT	B	3.00	9.0
BA 312	JUNIOR SEMINAR II.	A	1.00	4.0
BA 335	BUSINESS STATS	A	3.00	12.0
BA 337	BUSINESS LAW	B	3.00	9.0
BA 412	SENIOR SEMINAR II	A	1.00	4.0
MGT 430	BUSINESS POLICY	B	3.00	9.0
MKT 332	MARKETING RESEARCH	B	3.00	9.0
MKT 334	MARKETING CHANNELS	A	3.00	12.0

Undergrad	Attempt	Earned	Points	Divisor	GPA
Current Term	23.00	23.00	80.00	23.00	3.48
Cumulative	114.00	114.00	342.00	114.00	3.00

Spring semester 1998 grades.

At the conclusion of the semester I earned five As and four Bs, and successfully defended my senior thesis. The title of my study was, *Alcohol and Tobacco Target Marketing, Is It Good Business or Bad Ethics?* When I returned to school in the fall of 1998, it was the final semester of my undergraduate career. My class schedule consisted of Aerobics, Golf, Tennis, Bowling, and

Geography. Ultimately, taking all my most challenging core classes and saving my electives for the last semester of my senior year allowed me to graduate a semester earlier. I graduated December 4, 1998 and I moved back to Atlanta that same day. Since Benedict only had one commencement per year, I had to wait until the spring to actually march.

TISA

OK, WHAT'S NEXT?

The next morning, the day after I returned from South Carolina, I found myself staring at the very same walls I was staring at three and a half years ago. This is the very first time I can recollect experiencing a certain level of depression, but not in the traditional sense. My depression was caused by my transition. I thought I would have been more independent at that point in my life. I was trying to figure out what was next for me in this journey we call life. At that point I knew three things: I needed to get a job, I did not want to live in my parents' house, and there was more to life than what was inside I-285.

I-285 is an interstate that goes around the city of Atlanta. At the age of thirteen, my father explained to me that I should not just limit myself to my geographical location, and that there was more to life than what is inside 285. This is still one of my core philosophies. Shortly after being home for about three weeks, I figured out what was next for me and decided to join Omega Psi Phi, Fraternity Incorporated.

Certificate of Membership.

The Bruhs

Omega Psi Phi Fraternity, Inc. is the first international fraternal organization to be founded on the campus of a historically black college. It was founded on November 17, 1911, at Howard University in Washington, D.C. The founders were three Howard University undergraduates, - Edgar Amos Love, Oscar James Cooper and Frank Coleman. Joining them was their faculty adviser, Dr. Ernest Everett Just. From the initials of the Greek phrase meaning, "Friendship is essential to the soul," the name Omega Psi Phi was derived. That phrase was selected as the motto. Manhood, Scholarship, Perseverance and Uplift were adopted as Cardinal Principles. The official colors of the fraternity are royal purple and old gold. Members of Omega Psi Phi are traditionally known as "Omega Men," "Q Dogs," and "The Bruhs."

The first time I can remember seeing The Bruhs was in the winter of 1991, at Redan High School in Stone Mountain, a city outside of Atlanta. My best friend at that time, Jason and I decided to attend a step show at the school. I was fourteen and familiar with fraternities and sororities, but my exposure was not that extensive. Most of my exposure came from the AKA certificate, plaques, and other paraphernalia my mother had around the house. My mother pledged Alpha Kappa Alpha, Inc. in 1971 at Albany State University.

The Bruhs hanging out at the 3 Dollar Café.

All the fraternities and sororities were represented in the step show. As I watched the various fraternities and sororities perform, I thought it was pretty cool. The Alphas, Sigmas, and the Kappas stepped, but I was not really moved. Then all of a sudden, the lights went dim and a spotlight shined on this brother, dressed in purple and gold, wearing fatigues and gold boots. Next, I heard barking throughout the auditorium as about eight brothers started stepping (hopping) in a totally different way than the previous fraternities. It was a profound spectacle. Now, I didn't totally understand what I had witnessed, but I told myself that I wanted to be like those brothers and be a member of that fraternity.

ETA OMEGA SPR.99
"OUTLAW QUES"
Omega Psi Phi Fraternity - 100 Year Centennial
July 30, 2011
Howard University, Washington, DC

The OUTLAWS in D.C.

To become a member of Omega Psi Phi, either on the undergraduate or graduate level, certain requirements must be satisfied. During my years at Benedict College, I attempted to enter the world of Omega, but was unsuccessful in my endeavor. Ultimately, I graduated from college early and pursued Omega Psi Phi once I returned to Atlanta. Becoming a member of Omega Psi Phi was - and still is - highly competitive. I was able to pursue and gain membership into Omega Psi Phi Fraternity, Inc. on April 16, 1999. There were ten of us that were "made" that night and we were named the "10 OUTLAW Ques". This was one of my most challenging and greatest accomplishments. A month later, I returned to Benedict College for my commencement ceremony on May 9, 1999. Once again, I was left trying to figure out what was next.

With my parents at the Benedict College Graduation.

KUMI

AIR FORCE

In the summer of 1999, I was a college graduate, and a member of one the most prestigious organizations in the world at the age of twenty-two. However, I was working for the Internal Revenue Service, living with my parents, and I was unfulfilled, bored, and miserable. I knew that I was supposed to be doing more than just working a job and living with my parents. Before I knew it, my spirit led me to entertain the idea of joining the military. I know that sounds crazy. It sounded crazy to me as well! I was (and still am) one of the most rebellious people I know. I did not respect my parents' authority, so how could I adapt to military rules and regulations? My parents and friends had similar reactions once I shared the idea with them.

Still, I knew I had to shake things up in my life, because I believed I was destined for great things. I've always listened to people complain about their jobs, sitting in traffic, hating Monday mornings, and constantly anticipating Fridays and holidays. I refused to allow that to be my reality. I weighed my options and also discussed them with my father, who was retired military. The cons: I did not like people having control over my life, I did not agree with war and violence, and I was not the most patriotic person. The pros: I could go to school for free, I could take advantage of the Montgomery G.I. Bill, gain some needed structure and discipline, generate and save money, acquire various veteran benefits, and become self-sufficient.

After weighing the pros and cons and talking to my father, it was time for me to make a move. My father told me that the military was not a bad move, but the only branch I should consider was the Air Force. The reason he emphasized the Air Force was because he knew my personality and my quick temper. He warned, "If you join the Marines or Army and there is a war, you will most likely participate in that war." If you join the Navy, you will be on the water most of the time. If you go to the Air Force, you can concentrate on going to school. My father ended our conversation by saying, "You only have forty-eight months; you can do it." My mother said what she has always said, "I want you to do whatever you want to do in life, as long as it is not illegal or immoral."

After weighing my options and receiving my parents' blessings, I started preparing to "Aim High," which was the Air Force's motto. I also shared my plans with my inner circle of friends and my new line brothers. No one believed me. Everyone's response was basically, "Yea right! You going to the military? I will believe it when I see it!"

My response was, "Ok, don't say I didn't tell you."

AIR FORCE

Recruitment Process

I remember going to the recruiter's office and telling the recruiter that I wanted to join the Air Force and asking how soon could I leave. The recruiter explained the process and informed me that if I satisfied the requirements, I would be granted clearance to join the Air Force. The process consisted of presenting a high school diploma, passing a criminal background check, passing a complete physical, and first and foremost, receiving a high score on the Armed Services Vocational Aptitude Battery (ASVAB).

This was the second time in my life where I experienced something from my past coming back to haunt me. My parents used to always tell me, "Be careful of the things you do now, because it may affect you in the future." They were right. Remember that small incident I had in Cobb County? Well guess what popped up again when the Air Force recruiter ran my background check? My arrest from 1994! Luckily, since I was not convicted, it did not hurt my chances of entering the military. I passed my criminal background check with no problems, and received a high score on the ASVAB test.

As a result of my high score on the ASVAB, the recruiter informed me that I could just about pick any profession that the Air Force had to offer. She also gave me a date to report to the Military Entrance Processing Station (MEPS). The MEPS is the location designated to administer physicals, as well as finalize future recruits' occupations and dates to enter basic training.

♗ DELINQUENT TO DOCTOR

The night before I had to report to the MEPS, I was required to reside at a designated hotel with other future recruits. The purpose of housing all the recruits the night prior to reporting to MEPS was so that everyone would report to the correct location at the designated time. The next morning the arduous process of joining the Air Force continued with paperwork asking for demographic and background information and a complete physical to check for terminal illnesses, HIV, and current injuries.

Once that portion of the process was complete, it was time to choose my future Air Force Specialty Code (AFSC) in the Air Force. The Air Force Specialty Code (AFSC) is an alphanumeric code used by the United States Air Force to identify an Air Force Specialty. I had no idea what I wanted to do. I was walking blind.

In order to choose my AFSC, I had to meet with an Air Force recruiter at the MEPS. When I entered the recruiter's office, a coffee mug on the desk caught my eye because it was royal purple and old gold, which were the colors of my fraternity. Once I investigated and took a closer look, I found that the coffee mug read the symbols, "ΩΨΦ." My eyes lit up! I instantly inquired about the recruiter that owned the coffee mug. She explained that he was out for the day, but he would return on the next day. Of course, I preferred to discuss my options with the absent recruiter because of our fraternal affiliation. So I decided to return the next day.

When I returned the next day, my fraternity brother was sitting behind his desk. Once I entered the room, I immediately introduced myself not only as a new recruit, but also as a member of Omega Psi Phi, Inc. I was told that membership had its privileges, but this was the first time that I actually experienced the concept. Once we were acquainted, we began to discuss my future in the Air Force.

While he was looking through my military files, he came across my academic transcripts and discovered I had a Bachelor's Degree in Business Administration. Next he asked me if I would be interested in having a job in finance. I responded with an enthusiastic, "Yes, fo sho!" At this point, he instructed me to wait in the lobby, because he needed to do some research. I stayed in the waiting room and after about ten minutes he called me back in and I sat down.

"Check this out, I am not supposed to assign the Financial Analyst AFSC 6F031 to anymore recruits, but since you are the bruhs, I am going to hook you up."

"Cool, let's do it," I responded enthusiastically.

He explained to me that I would do six weeks of basic training at Lackland, Air Force Base in San Antonio, Texas. Next, I would do five weeks of Technical School at Sheppard Air Force Base, in Wichita Falls, Texas. Finally, I would report to my permanent duty station, which would be assigned to me once my technical training was complete.

"When do you want to leave?" he asked after I signed all the paperwork.

"Can I leave today?" I thought about it and then asked, "No, can I leave tomorrow? I need to say good-bye to my grandmother."

"No problem," he responded.

We shook hands and that was the last time we saw each other. Still, he was an intricate part of my military process, and inevitably my life.

When I left the MEPS, I went directly to my grandmother's house to tell her I was leaving. We had a brief conversation. After, I gave her a hug and told her that I would see her after I finished basic training. After leaving my grandmother's house, I went home to pack a small bag and told my parents and brother that I would see them after basic training as well. I reported to the same hotel where I stayed the night before going to the MEPS. I called a young lady that I was kicking it with at the time and asked her to drop me off at the hotel. I did not have a going away party, and I did not tell anyone, I just went away.

Basic Training

The next morning, I woke up at 5:00 a.m., ate breakfast, and boarded the bus for the MEPS. Once arriving at the MEPS, I realized that recruits from all over Georgia were meeting at this location to depart for basic training. All the recruits were accounted for and we loaded onto the bus, en route to Hartsfield

Jackson Airport. We first connected at O'Hare Airport in Chicago, Illinois before arriving in San Antonio, Texas.

Almost immediately, after walking off the plane, my basic training experience began. There was an Air Force representative waiting for us at the gate. He directed us to a holding area to wait for the bus that would transfer us to Lackland Air Force Base. While we were in this holding area, we were instructed to keep our mouths closed and not to move. After approximately thirty minutes, a military bus arrived outside the door of the holding area. The bus was a green version of a yellow school bus.

Next, two military training instructors (MTIs) entered the area. They immediately instructed us to gather our personal items and line up, and we were herded on to the bus like cattle. Again, we were told to stay silent and they gave us instructions on the when, what, and how, of what was about to take place. The number one instruction given by the training instructor was, "You are now the property of the United States Air Force and you are to follow all instructions by the training instructors and ranking officials without pause!"

We arrived at Lackland Air Force Base at approximately 1:00 a.m. We were ushered into what would be our living quarters for the next six weeks. Some people refer to military housing as dorms and some call them barracks. The dorm had two sides. Each side had two rows of single-sized beds. There were even some bunk beds. In all, there were about 120 beds in the dorm. When we arrived, recruits were already in the dorm asleep. We were each assigned a bed, locker, and trunk in the dark, instructed to go to sleep, and the MTIs left the dorm.

At about 4:30 a.m. that morning the military training instructors returned and all I remember hearing was a loud horn and screaming. I had only had about three hours of sleep. I woke up very disoriented and I thought I was in a dream. All I kept thinking was, "What in the world did I get myself into?" All the recruits who were there before my arrival got dressed in their military issued sweat pants and t-shirts and proceeded outside to satisfy their daily physical training requirements, which consisted of calisthenics and running. Since I was a new recruit, my first morning in the basic training was slightly different.

First, they took us down downstairs for breakfast. The MTI's literally gave us eight seconds to eat. Next, we acquired our military issued sweat suits, t-shirts, and shorts. All the items had Air Force branded on them. By the time we received our clothing, the other recruits had finished their morning physical training and were returning from breakfast. Once we returned to the dorm, we were met by recruits that were in their final week of basic training.

During the basic training process, exceptional recruits who were close to graduating from basic training were designated to assist with new recruits. Their assignment was to get those recruits acclimated to basic training. They gathered us into the day room in the dorm and instructed us to take the clothes we brought with us

106

and put them in a closet, to be stored until the end of our six weeks of training. While I was gathering my belongings and thoughts, one of the recruits in their sixth week approached me. Apparently, he noticed that I had on a purple shirt that read Omega Psi Phi. He expressed to me that his brother was a Q-Dog as well, and he had some advice for me. His advice was, "Don't try to be a super airman, only do what is required, and do not volunteer for anything, to avoid being assigned extra duties." I followed that advice throughout my Air Force career.

Weekly Training Schedule	
Week of Training (WOT) 1:	Reporting and saluting, Medical and Dental Appointments, GI Bill briefing, ID Cards, Dorm Guard Class, Career Guidance, Individual Drill, Dorm Preparation, and Haircuts.
WOT 2:	Personal Fitness, Dorm Inspection, Personal Appearance, Recognizing Military Insignia, Military Citizenship, Personal Interviews, Human Relations Class, and Flight Drill.
WOT 3:	Second Clothing issue, Dorm Inspection, Haircuts, Flight Drill, Air Force History and Organizational Structure, Fitness and Nutrition, Educational Opportunities, Enlisted Force History and Heritage, Environmental Awareness and Resource Protection, Sexual Harassment, and Chain of Command.
WOT 4:	Financial Management, Flight Pictures, Flight Drill, Military Citizenship, Career Progression, Enlisted Force Structure, Ethics, Core Values, and Air Force Rank Insignia.
WOT 5:	Law of Armed Conflict, Code of Conduct, Security, Confidence Course, Marksmanship training, Field Training Experience.
WOT 6:	Dorm Inspection, Hometown News Releases, Formal Retreat, Written test, Haircuts, Technical School Briefing, Commanders Departure Town Pass Briefing, Smoking Cessation, Orders Pick-up, and Graduation Parade.

Basic Training six-week schedule.

Over the next six weeks, my daily routine consisted of waking up at 4:30 a.m. and going to sleep at 9:00 p.m. Each morning consisted of calisthenics and running for thirty minutes. After morning physical training, we ate breakfast and then followed our itinerary for that day. Our daily activities included haircuts, vaccination shots, marching, the issuing of uniforms, taking classes on Air Force history, and getting prepared for Air Force life.

Air Force life was all about structure and avoiding negative consequences. If any recruit had areas of their training that were deficient, then that recruit would go through a process called, "recycling." Recycling was when a recruit had to go back a week or more in their training if they did not meet certain benchmarks. For example, we were required to hang and fold our clothes a certain way, and have them positioned a certain way in the closet and footlocker. The military training instructors conducted daily, random inspections to verify that we were meeting our benchmarks. If a recruit was in week five and they missed a benchmark, they could possibly go back to week four or week three.

Not only did we have to hang and fold our uniforms perfectly, we also had to make up our beds a certain way, keep the dorms spotless, run two miles under twenty minutes, complete a certain number of push-ups, sit-ups, and jumping jacks, learn how to march as a flight (group), and successfully pass a test on Air Force History. I am happy to say that I completed basic training in six weeks with no hiccups.

In keeping with tradition for the end of basic training, our flight was to design a flight t-shirt that denotes the personality of the flight. The brothers were not feeling the designs that our Caucasian counterparts were suggesting. All the examples of flight shirt designs we had seen illustrated white airmen. We were not down with that! Why should we have to wear white images? We were Black Airmen, and we wanted shirts that represented us, so we decided to design our own shirt. In addition, we wanted to pay homage to the Tuskegee Airmen (who were not mentioned in the Air Force history we had to learn).

In order for us to get the shirts made, we had to order a minimum of fifteen. Since our flight was predominately white, we asked some of the other brothers from other flights if they were interested in our idea. They absolutely loved it! We also asked some of the Caucasian airmen if they were interested in buying a shirt. They were mad because we wanted to do our own thing and declined. Our attitude was, "Whatever."

Our finished product was a black t-shirt, with three Tuskegee Airmen on the back walking out of fire, with two planes flying overhead. The front of the shirt had a plane on the left corner pocket, with "We on Fire!" under the picture of the plane. "We on Fire!" was a popular song by a group called the Hot Boys under Cash Money Records that we sang during our physical training sessions. Our flight leader, who was a brother, provided us with the artwork and a poem for the shirt. Overall, basic training was a

109

great experience. Then it was time to go to Technical School Training.

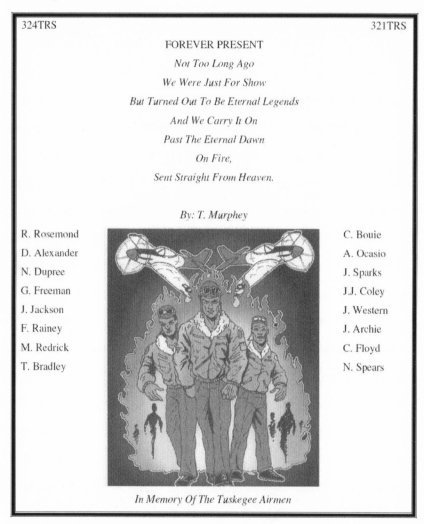

324TRS   321TRS

FOREVER PRESENT

Not Too Long Ago

We Were Just For Show

But Turned Out To Be Eternal Legends

And We Carry It On

Past The Eternal Dawn

On Fire,

Sent Straight From Heaven.

By: T. Murphey

R. Rosemond	C. Bouie
D. Alexander	A. Ocasio
N. Dupree	J. Sparks
G. Freeman	J.J. Coley
J. Jackson	J. Western
F. Rainey	J. Archie
M. Redrick	C. Floyd
T. Bradley	N. Spears

In Memory Of The Tuskegee Airmen

The back of our flight shirt.

During my last week of basic training, I received my orders for technical school. There were three Air Force bases designated for technical training: Lackland Air Force Base (where I was located at the time), Kessler Air Force Base, Biloxi, Mississippi, and Sheppard Air Force Base, Wichita Falls, Texas. For my particular AFSC, I was assigned to Sheppard Air Force Base, right outside of Dallas, Texas. Once I graduated from basic training, it was time for me to move on to the next stage of my Air Force journey which was tech school.

As a part of the last briefing process in our training, we had a chance to ask questions about tech school. We were basically told it was just like college. I was like, "Great, I had just left college, and I knew exactly what that was like." I was thinking girls, drinking, and parties. I was in for a rude awakening! The next morning after graduation, we boarded a charter bus en route to Wichita Falls. We were on the bus for approximately six hours. When we arrived at Sheppard Air Force Base, my assumptions of a college life experience and the reality of tech school did not match.

Technical School

When we stepped off the bus, we were met by what seemed like more military training instructors (MTIs). I thought MTIs only existed in basic training. These individuals were screaming at us and instructed us to line up with our luggage. I was very confused, because I thought tech school was going to be like college life. I was so outside of my basic training frame of mind that I got in trouble for not following instructions. To be honest, I was looking at them like they were crazy. Once I gained my bearings, I fell in line in order to get further instructions pertaining to my living quarters and daily itinerary for the upcoming weeks. After the preliminary introductions of the dorm sergeants, we were assigned to our rooms (which we shared with another airman) and we were given a tour of the base. After the tour, we ate dinner and retired to our dorm room.

The United States Air Force

CERTIFIES THAT

AB MACK R ROSEMOND
FR260279502

HAS SUCCESSFULLY COMPLETED THE
Basic Military Training Course, LMABM9T000, 6 Weeks
(Initial Nuclear, Biological, Chemical Defense (NBCDF) Training, Self Aid-and-Buddy Care,
Law of Armed Conflict, and Anti-Terrorism
AND IS HEREWITH AWARDED THIS

Certificate of Training

Dean G. Fox
DEAN G FOX Major, USAF
Commander

08-Nov-99
DATE

AF FORM 1256, NOV 66 Previous edition will be used.

Basic Training certificate.

The next morning, we were ordered to report to a designated area so that we could be given information on the rules, protocol, and overview of our technical school process. The most highlighted feature of technical school was the phase system. There were three phases in the phase system. During Phase One, airmen had to keep their uniforms on twenty-four hours a day, we could not leave the base, and we had to be in the dorm by 9:00

112

p.m. daily. During Phase Two, we could change to our civilian clothes after we left our training class, we had a 9:00 p.m. daily curfew, and we could leave the base on the weekend, but we had to wear our dress blues uniform. During Phase Three, we were able to wear our civilian clothes after class, didn't have a curfew, and could leave the base during the week after we finished school and weekends. I did not remember college being like that, but I sucked it up and moved on.

The next six weeks of technical training consisted of getting up everyday for roll call, marching to class in flight formation, and sitting in class for eight hours, just like a 9 to 5 job. Once we finished class, we had to report to the flight line for physical training. Once I reached Phase Three, life at Sheppard Air Force Base was more like college life. Also, during Phase Three was when I entered the last part of my training. During the last weeks of training, I was given orders for my permanent duty station. The orders I received indicated that my permanent duty station would be the San Bernardino OPLOC, in San Bernardino, California. This was not a traditional Air Force Base, but an operational location. It was more like an office park. I asked myself, "Where in the hell is San Bernardino?"

Initially, I was not interested in going to San Bernardino. I wanted to go oversees. The powers that be stated that we could trade orders with each other, as long as the AFSC and graduation date were the same and we completed the process within the next two weeks from the date our orders were issued. Luckily, I found a brother with the same AFSC and graduation date to change with me. His orders indicated that he was on his way to Kadena Air Force Base in Okinawa, Japan. However, he preferred to stay stateside. It was a win-win situation. Everything was going as planned, until he decided to get married to a chick he had only known for a few weeks. I said, "Motherfucker!" I was pissed!

I'm not sure about today's military, but back then, many members of the Air Force would get married soon after meeting. As a result, my plans of going to Japan were derailed because when military members marry each other during the process of receiving transfers to other bases, orders have a tendency to change. Unfortunately for me, that airman and his new wife both received new orders.

With the two-week deadline coming to a close, I started preparing myself for San Bernardino, CA. During my preparation, representatives from San Bernardino assigned me a mentor to guide me through my transition from tech school to my permanent duty station. California natives told me that San Bernardino was a beautiful city surrounded by snowcapped mountains. I was intrigued.

In preparation for my move, I made sure I put every single check in a savings account, which I had been doing since basic training. My logic was that I had free room and board, and I was provided access to three square meals a day. There was no reason why I should spend money excessively. I was also aware that I would have to find transportation and lodging once I arrived to San Bernardino. I had to find an apartment because there were no barracks or dorms at the OPLOC. I requested that my mentor send me an apartment guide and information on local car dealerships. I wanted to make sure that I did my research prior to getting to the west coast.

During the final couple of weeks of my technical school training, I was able to explore Dallas, and meet a whole new circle of associates. I also finished technical school successfully. The day after graduation, I was granted eight days to report to my permanent duty station in San Bernardino. I returned to Atlanta to prepare for my new life in the "Wild, Wild, West."

The transition from technical school to my permanent duty station was easy. The Air Force granted me eight days of personal leave, an allowance to pay for airline tickets, a daily per diem, and they paid moving expenses from Atlanta, GA to San Bernardino, CA. During my time at home, I went to Benedict to attain copies of my transcript for the purpose of enrolling into a graduate program once I settled in San Bernardino. I packed bags and boxes to be picked up by a moving company designated by the military and also visited with a few childhood friends. This was one of the major times in life that I realized I was not missing anything at home. Even though I knew moving out to California was going to be different, new, and at some times, scary, I was eager to experience new adventures in a new world. After saying my last good-byes, I was out.

SHEPPARD A.F.B. WICHITA FALLS, TEXAS

Technical School class photo.

San Bernardino

At this point in my life, my travel experience was very limited. I had never been to the West Coast before, so I had no idea what to expect. The flight was four hours, and I thought it was the longest flight in the world! My flight arrived at the Ontario Airport, in Ontario, CA which is the closest airport to San Bernardino. I was met at the airport by my mentor Allen and another airman that was a good friend of his. Allen and his friend were both Caucasian, which was not a problem, but it was different. I had never hung out, or kept company with anyone that looked or acted different then me. My new adventure had officially begun.

On the drive from the airport to San Bernardino, we were all in the car getting acquainted with each other. I was sharing with them my experience in the Air Force up until that point, and they were letting me know what I should expect in my new environment. Once we arrived at Allen's apartment, he made sure that I settled in, we talked for a while, and he said he would take me to meet my superiors the following morning. The next morning, I woke up and looked out the window. I was surrounded by the snowcapped mountains that people told me about. Once I was dressed, Allen took me to the San Bernardino OPLOC to meet my superiors and new coworkers.

The OPLOC was nothing like a traditional military base; it was more of an office park that had more civilians than military members. I was given a tour of the installation and I was able to meet some of the airmen I would be working with, as well as my immediate supervisor. Everyone seemed very friendly and helpful. My supervisor informed me that I had a week to find transportation and housing. Since I had already done my research prior to arriving in San Bernardino, I had a jump on my immediate task.

I knew that I had limited funds to work with; therefore I had to be smart about how much I spent. When looking for an apartment, my criteria consisted of price, location, and cleanliness. Within forty-eight hours I found the perfect spot around the corner from the military installation at Summit Place Apartments. It was a gated community, a five-minute drive from my job, and the rent was only $445 per month. The only thing left to do was find transportation. My criteria for the purchase of a new car included price, reliability, and safety. Within that same two-day period, I purchased a 2000 Mazda Protégé for approximately $15,000, which I paid off in two years. I'm still driving the same car to this day (twelve years later).

Once I settled into my new job and community, I enrolled at California State University San Bernardino (CSUSB). I majored in Marketing and Communication. My daily schedule consisted of going to work from 6:00 a.m. to 3:00 p.m., and going to class in the evenings. Initially, I did not like California, because I think I was just used to southern living. My biggest complaint was that there were no Waffle Houses on the west coast. I had to learn how to embrace not only different people, but also different environments and experiences as I was entering into manhood.

3% Body Fat

It was a very interesting time in my life. I was living in a new state, with a new job, and in graduate school. Along with the aforementioned experiences, California also had a very profound impact on my fitness, health, and diet. In addition to waking up in the California sun, my younger brother also proved to be a great catalyst in igniting my healthy lifestyle change.

AIR FORCE

Maurice came to visit me one week prior to September 11, 2001. It had been a while since I had actually seen him. When he came to visit me, I noticed that he had been working out a whole lot. I was very impressed. I was so impressed, that I thought, "I can't have my little brother looking better than me." The following Monday after my brother left I met with the personal trainer, Guillermo Escalante, who trained me on-site at the OPLOC. I told him I wanted a bigger chest, arms, shoulders, and legs and I also wanted six pack abs. He told me that 75% of working out was having the proper diet. At that time I was consuming cheese burgers, fried chicken, Oreos, Chicken Alfredo, Kool-Aid, soda, and countless other unhealthy items.

Guillermo told me that I would not be successful if I did not get my diet together. He told me that I should go home and throw out all the unhealthy foods. After disposing of the unhealthy foods, I incorporated healthier items, such as baked fish and chicken, brown rice, green vegetables, fruit, and plenty of water. My workout regiment consisted of one hour of cardio (running/cycling) per day and I broke down each muscle of my body once per week. I was also instructed to eat at least six meals a day and drink at least one gallon of water, which would assist in increasing my metabolism and ultimately help me burn calories.

With the structure of being in the Air Force, inspiration from my brother, and living in sunny California, I was able to stop eating unhealthy foods "cold turkey," and made a lifestyle change.

This was another great challenge in my life. With a laid-back position and a cool supervisor, I was able to workout for two hours daily during my lunch hour. I was so addicted to working out, that I found myself depressed if I could not make it to the gym. On the days I couldn't go, I would run around my apartment complex. I followed my diet and work out regiment 100% of the time.

Triathlon at Lake Lanier.

Over a period of three months, I went from 19% body fat to 10% body fat, and put on ten pounds of muscle. My trainer was so impressed with my progress that he suggested I enter into an amateur bodybuilding contest. At first, I was like, "No! Man that is gay! I am not putting on those little draws." He simply laughed and said, "I will pay for your registration and sign you up."

Scuba diving in Miami, Florida.

Basically, his suggestion became a reality. Before I knew it, I went from working out for my own personal goals to training for an amateur bodybuilding competition. Over the next three months, I went from 10% body fat to 3% body fat, gained an additional ten pounds of muscle, and we were on our way to the competition. The bodybuilding competition was in Chico, which was in northern

California. I was not just the only African male in the competition, but it seemed like I was the only African in the whole town. Unfortunately, I did not place in the competition. However, my trainer and I were very proud of my progress, which was the same as winning in my book. In addition to the goals I met, the lifestyle change I engineered is still prevalent in my everyday life today. Presently, I am an avid runner, cyclist, scuba diver, swimmer, and body builder. I also follow a fairly strict diet.

With Guillermo at my first bodybuilding competition.

In the process of preparing for my bodybuilding competition, I was still an active duty airman in the Air Force, and I was a full-time graduate student. Now, I do not want you to think it was all work and no play while I was in San Bernardino. That was definitely not the case. While living on the west coast, I was able to frequently visit Las Vegas, Los Angeles, Palm Springs, San Francisco, and Tijuana, Mexico. It was a great time of self-discovery. I did not particularly like the military, but I loved living in California. I even got the opportunity to meet one of my heroes, Dr. John Carlos!

John Carlos

John Carlos is a former Olympic track and field athlete known for his black power salute on the podium with Tommy Smith at the 1968 Olympic Games in Mexico City, Mexico. While attending CSUSB, I participated in various community service projects as a student and member of my fraternity. I believed that the community service projects that I participated in were of great importance, but not sufficient enough. I thought I could be doing a lot more. I wanted to orchestrate a community service project on a higher level, so I started searching.

One day, I saw Dr. Carlos being interviewed on television. He was talking about his life story and what he was currently doing. I was so intrigued that I went online to research him and discovered his phone number on a website. I decided to call the number and left a message. My main purpose was to find out how I could purchase a picture of the historical black power salute from the 1968 Mexico City Olympics. The next day I came home, looked through my caller I.D. and saw the name John Carlos. I thought, "Yea right!" I called the number back. A man answered the phone.

"May I speak to Mr. Carlos?"

"This is he," responded the man on the other end of the phone.

I was stunned for a moment, because I could not believe it was him. I introduced myself and told him how much I admired him for what he did in 1968. After talking for a while, I asked him if we could meet in person. His reply was, "You know, I don't usually do this, but why don't you come out to the house and we can talk. I have a good feeling about you." Since he lived in a neighboring city about an hour away, I told him I was en route.

We talked for hours about everything including politics, education, civil rights, world affairs, family, and about what really happened in 1968. He said the black athletes were initially going to boycott the games all together, but they ultimately decided to take a different approach to protest the fact that black people were deemed good enough to compete and win medals for the United States, but not valuable enough to be treated with dignity and equality in their own country. Their approach was a silent protest to let the world know about the struggle black people were facing in America. I asked him if they took his medal. He responded, "No! That was just propaganda created to prevent other black athletes from displaying other forms of protest."

John Carlos and Tommy Smith, 1968 Olympics, Mexico City.

Before I left, I asked him if he would be interested in coming to speak at my school. He said he would love to do it, and to just let him know what the details were. A month later, I arranged for Dr. Carlos to speak at CSUSB before students, faculty, staff and the media. It was a wonderful event and we have been great friends since then.

With Dr. Carlos at his house.

AIR FORCE 🔥

Time to Go

With a year and half left in my enlistment, my immediate supervisor approached me, and asked me if I was interested in getting out of the Air Force before my four-year enlistment expired. I responded a resounding "Hell Yes!" In the summer of 2002, the Air Force was downsizing and closing down all the Operational Locations (OPLOCs) throughout the Air Force, and San Bernardino was at the top of the list. His next question was, "When do you want to get out?" I told him to give me a couple of days and I would get back with him. I had to evaluate and examine two things: First, I still had a few months before graduating from my Master's program. Secondly, I had to research how getting out of the Air Force early would affect my veteran's benefits.

Once I did my research and found out that I would qualify for 100% full veteran's benefits if I served at least thirty-six months in the military, it was time to make a decision. At that point in my enlistment, I was at thirty-one months. I was one month away from graduation and five months away from qualifying for my full benefits. It was the month of August and I reported to my supervisor. I initially told him that I wanted to be discharged in February of 2003. My plan was to graduate with my Master's, satisfy my thirty-six months, and save some money. Once I graduated a month later, I started getting anxious, and February looked like it was ten years away. I was ready to get out ASAP! I decided to change my date to December 15, 2002.

Hiking on Big Bear Mountain.

Once I finalized my exit date, I started preparing for the next phase in my life. I submitted a letter to my landlord indicating my departure at the end of November. I asked a friend if I could stay with her for a few days, before leaving to go back to Atlanta. I made arrangements with a moving company to move my furniture, and arranged for my best friend Buster to fly to California to help me drive my car to Georgia. I was released from the Air Force on December 6, 2002 and Buster and I were back in Atlanta by December 8th. We drove from Los Angeles to Atlanta in thirty-six hours straight. A new chapter in my life was about to begin.

**With my mother at the
California State University San Bernardino Graduation.**

To this day, many people ask me, "What in the world made me go to the Air Force?" My short answer is that I was bored and I needed to shake up my life. I also explain that I entered the Air

129

Force with an exit strategy already planned. I tell people no matter what situation or relationship you are in - I do not care if it is school, a job, boyfriend, girlfriend or family members - there should be what I call "equitable benefit." If you are not benefiting equally or more in any situation or relationship, you should not be in that situation or relationship. Therefore, I knew that the Air Force had a plan for me, and I knew that they were going to pimp me as much as they could. My plan was to pimp them just as much, or more.

The California State San Bernardino Campus.

I was able to complete my master's degree for free, save money, pay off my car, travel up and down the west coast, visit Mexico, and meet a new circle of friends. Even more, I became a

United States Veteran with full benefits, including approximately $38,000 in G.I. Bill money for school, which I still use to this day.

Last day in the Air Force at Edwards Air Force Base.

KUMI NA MOJA

CHOICES

The morning after returning to Atlanta, I found myself sleeping in the same bed I slept in when I was five years old. Once again, I pondered, "What am I going to do next?" The only thing that I was certain of was that I was going to be able to take advantage of an unemployment check for the next six months as a part of my discharge arrangements. For the next couple of months I fell into a deep depression. I would sleep all day and night. I only ventured out of the bed to eat, shower, or use the bathroom.

Apparently, I was delusional and thought that just because I was a veteran and I had my Master's Degree that it was going to be easy street once I returned to Atlanta. Obviously, that was not the case. My depression was seemingly so bad that my father came in my room one day and said, "You can't find a job sleeping in the bed everyday." (Translation: You better start making some choices and create some options for yourself, because you cannot live here forever.) My father's gesture of encouragement offered me a modicum of motivation.

CHOICES

Tired of "Being Pimped"

This motivation led me to pursue a position with the Internal Revenue Service (IRS) for the second time in life as a Financial Analyst. The first time I worked for the IRS was in 1999 when I was pursuing Omega Psi Phi. I did not like it then, so why did I think I was going to like it a second time around almost four years later? Nonetheless, I needed a job, and the IRS was accessible to me. When you start most jobs, there is a training period and the IRS was no different. I remember coming in every morning at 7:30 a.m. and having to sit in a room and listen to a proctor instruct me on how to execute a job I did not want to do.

I had never liked working a 9 to 5 job. Up until that point, I had about thirty jobs in my life. I've been employed by Pizza Hut, Fort Gillem Commissary, Hardee's, ProSport, Jarman's Shoes, Amvets, Baker's Shoes, Checkers, Wendy's, Taco Bell, TJ Maxx, JC Penny's, Nation's Bank, Bell South Marketing, Wackenhut Securities, Lerner New York, Bath and Body Works, and the Air Force, just to name a few. I had the bulk of those jobs when I was in high school and college. My motto was, "If a job is not fun, throw up the deuces and find a new gig." The longest I kept a job was when I was in the Air Force, which was three years, two months, and twenty-three days. My grandmother used to be able to sense when I was going to leave a particular job. When I would leave for work, she would say to my mother, "Carolyn I think he

133

has that look in his eyes, I think he will be home early tonight."
And sure enough, I came home early.

The IRS was definitely a job that I did not enjoy from the
beginning. Everyday was the same routine: getting up every
morning at 5:00 a.m., sitting in traffic for an hour, starting a
training class at 7:30 a.m., taking a break at 9:30 a.m., going back
to training, having lunch at 11:30 a.m., back to class at 12:30 p.m.,
another break at 2:00 p.m., and finally getting off work at 4:00
p.m. to sit in traffic again. The next day, I would wake up and do
the same thing all over again. I was definitely not having fun.

One day during training, while listening to another boring
section of an IRS manual, I was inspired to write down what was
on my mind. Now, I want you to understand that I had never
written any poetry in my life. But for what ever reason I was
inspired to write. All of a sudden this indescribable feeling came
over me. I inwardly proclaimed, "I feel like I am being pimped."
And I started writing. When I finished, I had created a one-page
poem called, "Being Pimped." Shortly thereafter, I put the Internal
Revenue Service in my rearview mirror. Even though I had a
tendency to walk away from jobs, I always continued to make
options for myself. I firmly believe then, as I do now, that if you
don't make your own choices, someone else will make a choice for
you.

Being Pimped

Being Pimped is a child of the sun being kidnapped and thrown in a land of snow.

Being Pimped is having to work for someone they didn't even know.

Being Pimped is building a nation with your blood, sweat and tears, but having to live enslaved physically and mentally, year after year after year......

Being Pimped is selling drugs to your own people and throwing up colors, then end up behind bars while they laugh and say "look at those stupid, ignorant brothers".

Being Pimped is running, jumping, dancing and singing for a small amount of money, while your owner enjoys most of the milk and honey.

Being Pimped is buying name brand clothes you can't afford to possess, thinking that your education is less important than how you dress.

Being Pimped is not knowing you're ignorant, living a life that wasn't meant, even worse being aware of your ignorance and remaining complacent.

WAKE UP!!!

-- Dr. Abdalla Rashad Tau

My only poem.

Real Estate License

In the early 2000s, the real estate market was booming and there were a great number of people acquiring real estate licenses. Since I was in limbo at the time and not really knowing what my next move was going to be, I decided to jump on the realtor bandwagon and pursue a real estate license myself. Various schools offered classes to prepare for the real state exam. I decided to attend the Georgia MLS Training Institute.

My real estate license certificate.

The Georgia MLS Training Institute offered three types of class formats: day classes, evening classes, or online classes. The salesperson pre-license course covered three areas which were terms and concepts, finance, and contracts. Since I was like Tommy from the show *Martin* (NO JOB), I elected to take day classes, which allowed me to successfully complete the program in four weeks because we were in class from 9 to 5, five days a week. After I completed the program, I was eligible to take the state real estate test. On April 2, 2003 I passed my real estate exam with a total score of 84.9%. Within a couple of weeks I attained my license, and started working with a real estate company called Phoenix Properties out of Decatur. Once again, I reached another pinnacle, still searching for my next high.

Personal Training

Shortly after, I found my next high. I had only been back in Atlanta for four months. Many of my friends from high school had not seen me since high school, which was eight years prior to 2003. The reoccurring reaction to me was, "Wow! Have you been working out?" and "What did you do to get in such good shape?" I found myself giving advice on diet and fitness. I was having discussions on diet and working out so frequently that I concluded that I might be able to make some money of my knowledge. I started searching for a personal training certification program.

I researched many programs, but they were all online. I have always hated on-line classes; I preferred human interaction, even today. After chatting with a personal trainer from Bally's Fitness, I enrolled in the World Instructional Training Schools (WITS) training program. I attended classes on Saturdays and Sundays at a Bally's Fitness Location during the six week course. WITS provided a compact twenty-four hour training course of core knowledge and hands on training in exercise physiology, nutrition, biomechanics, and practical application. After completing the course work, I had to pass a written test as well as complete a

137

demonstration of the personal training skills I had attained. I satisfied both requirements almost effortlessly.

My personal training certificate.

I officially became a certified personal trainer on August 3, 2003. After discussions with my father about my newly acquired license and certification, we agreed that I needed to take steps toward entrepreneurship. He told me that I should create two separate corporations and to make sure I did not commingle funds. That year I created two businesses: *The Rosemond Group Reality Inc.* and *Optimal Personal Fitness, LLC.* I opened two separate business accounts and had two separate credit cards for each entity.

This was a time of great accomplishments for me, but I was still unfulfilled.

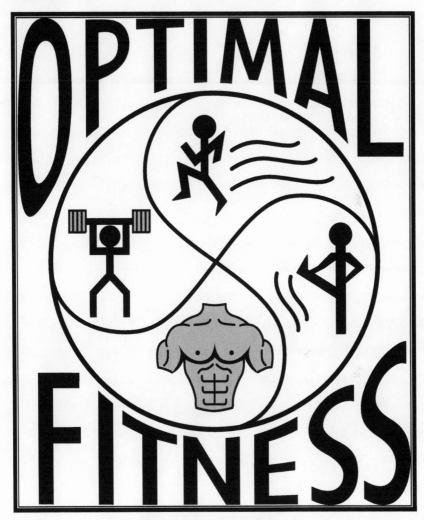

The Optimal Personal Fitness Logo.

As a result of my accomplishments, my routine of depression and daily sleeping subsided some, but continued until I received a phone call from my sister-from-another-mother, Nicole. She asked me to accompany her to a job fair.

"What type of job fair?" I asked.

"A teacher's job fair."

"But I am not a teacher."

"It doesn't matter. I am coming to get you!"

So I got out of the bed, took a shower, and put on a suit. I also printed a few copies of my resume and ventured off to the job fair with Nicole. The fair was held at the Civic Center in downtown, Atlanta.

Once we arrived, we went our separate ways. Nicole's educational background was middle school math and language arts. My background was business education. I maneuvered through the different schools, only seeking out the schools that were interested in business education teachers. Once I exhausted all my options, I waited for Nicole until she was finished networking and I returned home. The job fair was on a Thursday and on the following Monday morning I received a phone call from the human resources coordinator for middle school and high school teachers.

She introduced herself and proceeded to ask me if I was interested in having a teaching position. I had been unemployed for about five months, so my reply was an emphatic, "Yes!" Next, she asked me a series of questions pertaining to my teaching background. She asked me if I had a current teaching certificate, had ever taught, taken any education classes, or completed an on-line application for Turner County Schools. The answer was, "No" for every single question. With that being said, she suggested if I was interested in the field of education, I should fill out an on-line application and also entertain the idea of substitute teaching, so that I could get some experience in the classroom setting. I immediately began the process of entering the world of public school education.

KUMI NA MBILI

JOE CLARK

I had never thought about being a teacher in my life. However, once I came home from the Air Force and started having various conversations with high school friends and other peers about the field of education, my interest was sparked. I remember one conversation with an associate in particular.

"Rashad, with the way you think, you should be a teacher."

"What do you mean?" I asked.

"You have a very unique way of looking at life."

They further said that I could be a positive influence on today's "off-the-chain" children. So, that conversation coupled with my job fair experience, launched my teaching experience.

Substitute Teaching

My grocery list of things to do on the road of attaining my teaching certification consisted of filling out the on-line application, finding a business education vacancy, and finding a teaching certification program. While searching for a teaching position and a certification program, I entered the world of substitute teaching.

JOE CLARK

My first substitute teaching experience was at Quigley High School in the fall of 2003. The morning that I entered the office of Quigley High School, I informed the secretary that I was there to sub for a science class. The secretary's response was a statement and question, "I understand you are here for one position, but do you mind taking over the band class?" Now mind you, I had not been in a high school classroom since 1995, so I had no idea what to expect. Naively, I said, "Sure I will take the position for the day." I had no idea what I was getting myself into. I signed in, I was given my instructions for the day, and I was on my way.

When I entered the band room, I thought, "What the fuck is going on?" First of all, there were approximately 90 students in the band room and they were doing everything but band related activities. There were students shooting dice, playing tunk (cards), listening to I-pods, eating Hot Cheetos, kissing in the corner, using profanity, and tussling. Let's just say it was complete chaos. Now, you have to understand that I was twenty-six and I looked young for my age. I was also dressed very casual that day, so the students were trying to figure out if I was a student or a teacher. I sat back and assessed the situation for about two minutes. I told myself, beyond anything else, "I am an adult and they are children. It's time to take control."

I immediately looked for the young male lion in the room. Fortunately, the young brother I chose just happened to be one of the band's drum majors, which was a student the children were

143

used to being led by. I informed him who I was and what I wanted him to do. I told him to get about five other brothers to take the chairs that were stacked on the walls and create five rows in a lecture auditorium style. I also told him to let them know I was the substitute teacher for the day and to sit down. Once I finished with my instructions, I stood on a two-foot platform, in the front of the classroom and quietly stared at every single student in the room. I did not say a word. I did not make any facial expressions, just a very stern stare.

The expressions on their faces showed their confusion. They were trying to figure out exactly who and what they were dealing with. My thinking was that I had survived the most challenging pledging process in the world, and made it through military basic training, so this situation was nothing in comparison. Also, they were children! Once everyone was seated, I proceeded to introduce myself. I told them that my name was Mr. Rosemond and I was their substitute teacher for the day. Next I told them, "I see that you like to talk, that's fine, but we are going to have an organized conversation." I informed them that we could talk about anything as long as they were respectful. I asked them if they were cool with my plan and they responded with a collective, "Yes!"

I told them that I would introduce myself first and give a little about my background, they would give their introduction and background, and then they could ask me any question they desired. There were two other adults in the vicinity, a classroom teacher down the hall, and the in-school suspension administrator next door. Once the students and I started getting engaged in the conversation, it went surprisingly well. The students were quiet, respectful, and they raised their hands if they had any questions or comments. The only interruptions I experienced were from the two other adults in the area.

In between class changes, I talked to the other two teachers and asked them why they came into the classroom looking frantic. They both said the same thing, "We have never seen those students that disciplined and respectful." They were in complete disbelief. At the end of the day, I went to the front office to sign out and one of the teachers came into the office as I was leaving. She told the principal that she should hire me, because she had never seen a teacher handle a group of students how I handled the students in the band room. That was the day I realized teaching and helping others was my calling. Ironically, this was around the same time I stopped using profanity, I stopped consuming alcohol, and I stopped referring to my brothers (African Men) as niggers. However, becoming a teacher was not the only variable that caused me to stop those behaviors in my life.

No Profanity, Drinking, or Niggaz

There was a time when profanity was a constant in my daily conversations. I used to playfully call women "bitches" and "hoes." It was not a good day unless I said "Motherfucker" at least four times a day. I remember feeling very violent and angry when I used certain profane words. I realized that words are very powerful. I did not want to feel angry anymore, therefore I decided to stop.

As far as calling my brothers "niggers," it started not to make sense to me anymore. How could I possibly advocate for the betterment of my race if I consistently referred to my people by a term used by our oppressors to demean and degrade us? It seemed counterproductive. So, instead of calling my brothers and sisters "niggaz," I started referring to them as "brother" and "sister."

I also stopped drinking, because I just did not find any benefit in drinking anymore. Let's examine the pros and the cons. I see absolutely no pros to drinking. The cons: an unnecessary expense and it was unhealthy. Ultimately, I believe I stopped these activities because as a person who was cultivating young minds and being charged to help others, I also needed to address my personal deficiencies.

First Position

I continued to sub for about another year. In August of 2004, I was preparing to fly out to Los Angeles to attend my line brother's wedding. I received a phone call from the human resources administrator the day before I was supposed to fly out. She asked me if I wanted a job. I told her yes. She instructed me to come to the Turner County School System Headquarters. Once I arrived, she explained to me that a Business Education position was open at Newton High School and she was offering me the position. She also added that I had to report to pre-planning the following day. Pre-planning is when teachers have to report to school, prior to the students arriving to plan for the school year.

I told her that I definitely wanted to take the position, but I had plans to leave for Los Angeles the next morning. She said she understood, and I could start work when I returned to Atlanta the following Monday. She also instructed me to go by the school, meet my new principal, Mr. Jefferson, and gather some materials that could prepare me for my first day of school. When I met with my future supervisor and shared my situation with him, he was not too enthused. He suggested that I cancel my arrangements and report to work the following day. Once I left the school, I called the human resources supervisor and I told her about my encounter with Mr. Jefferson. She told me, "Do not worry about what he said. It's unfair for him to require that you go to work tomorrow, because you were just hired today. Go to L.A., have fun, and we will see you on Monday." Needless to say, my future principal was not happy with the decision.

After a great weekend of sun and fun, I returned to Atlanta right on time for my first day of school. I jumped right in as if I had been teaching forever. The kids responded to me right away. Not only did I teach the kids about business education, I also discussed life, and the importance of becoming self-sufficient. Most of our discussions were related to my life as a delinquent adolescent growing up in Decatur and how I overcame my delinquent behavior to become a productive adult. My aim was not only to educate, but also to inspire. Compared to other teachers, my teaching style was - and still is - quite unorthodox.

I patterned my teaching style after Joe Clark. Joe Clark was a principal from Paterson, New Jersey that inspired the making of the movie *Lean on Me,* starring Morgan Freeman. He was a principal that took a school that was totally dysfunctional and turned it around, using a very nonconformist style. Joe Clark demanded excellence and did not accept excuses. He was more concerned about the students and the community and less about the bureaucracy of the public school system. I definitely had Joe Clark in my veins. When I walked in a classroom, my motto was, "This is not a democracy. This is dictatorship." For the purpose of establishing structure and discipline to educate the student, my methods worked perfectly. With the way I came into the position, and me not following the script written by the principal, I was not his favorite person.

Ultimately, we locked horns on occasion about my teaching style and he wanted me to change. My attitude was quite nonchalant, and I wanted to do my own thing. Our relationship came to a boil when we had a disagreement over me giving consequences to students for calling each other niggers. I forbade that language in my classroom. My feeling was if a white student used that language toward a black student, it would be an issue. I wanted my students to understand it was unacceptable for anyone to use it.

One day I was summoned to his office to discuss why I was giving children detention and sending discipline referrals to the assistant principals for students calling each other niggers. I explained to him that it was a racial slur and it was unacceptable. I also pointed out that using racial slurs was against county rules. His reply was, "Mr. Rosemond we have to accept the fact that the word is a part of our youth culture." I did not agree, but I was tired of being in the office. So I said ok and I left.

The next day, after having a night to think about the situation, I e-mailed Mr. Jefferson to express my discontent with his opinion. Needless to say, he was not very happy. As a result of my actions, he put me on a Professional Development Plan (PDP). A PDP is a plan which consists of a series of requirements supervisors require teachers to satisfy if they feel their work ethic is not sufficient. When he presented me with the PDP, I told him, "The only way that I would complete that PDP, if Yeshua (Jesus' real name) came down from the heavens, tapped me on my left shoulder and told me to complete it," and I walked out if his office. Since I was not only an employee of Turner County, but also a product of Turner County, I knew people who worked for the district in important positions and I started working on my plan to get out of my situation.

149

My cause was also bolstered because the human resource supervisor really liked me as a teacher and as a person. She really wanted to see me succeed. As I was going through my situation, a brand new school was in the process of being built in Turner County and I was strategizing how I could attain the school's business education position. I had to figure out how to get out of my dilemma unscathed. Eventually, I found myself back at the county office with the human resource supervisor discussing my future as an educator in the public school system.

During our meeting, we discussed the issue at hand, as well as possible remedies. Ironically, the principal that was opening the new school was one of my fraternity brothers that I had known for a while. Next, she asked me three questions.

"Would you like me to transfer you to King High School with Dr. Anders?" was her first question.

"Yes."

"What are we going to do about this PDP?" was her next question.

"To be honest, I am going to tell you the same thing I told Mr. Jefferson, 'the only way I am going to complete that PDP is if Yeshua comes down from the heavens, taps me on my left shoulder, and tells me to complete the PDP,'" I answered.

"Well that's not going to happen, is it?" she asked with a slight chuckle.

"No."

"Can you last at your school until the end of the semester?" she asked third.

"Yes."

After the semester was over, I was on my way to King High School.

Second Position

I was very thankful to the human resource supervisor and Dr. Anders for rescuing me from my situation. My time at Newton High School was not a complete wash. As a first year teacher with a Master's Degree in Business, and a 3.2 GPA, I qualified to enroll into the Alternative Teaching Certification Program. Even with all my drama I was experiencing, I was progressing in my certification program effortlessly.

Once I arrived at King High School, I instantly found myself in a great situation. First of all there were a high number African males on staff, and a great percentage of them were members of Omega Psi Phi, including the head principal, head police officer, band director, chorus teacher, math teacher, the entire football team staff, and myself. There was a very high level of discipline and structure throughout the school. Not only that, my teaching strategy and my personality matched the principal's approach to handling students as well. This was a great environment for students to learn and I enjoyed coming to work everyday.

Even though I liked my job, the urge for me to live in another country emerged. I continued to satisfy the requirements for my teaching certification, but I also started researching programs abroad. Through my research, I came across the Japanese Exchange and Teaching Program (JET Program). I started the application process immediately. By the end of the school year, I was in the last stages of the interview process and taking the last classes of my teaching certification - It was time to make some decisions. Unbeknownst to me, I was not supposed to be at King in the first place, and a plan was put in place for me to be transferred.

Fortunately, I was accepted into the JET Program and I started preparing for a new life in the Far East. I finished my teaching certification requirements in the designated time given. I was able to get out of my teaching contract, because the district viewed this experience as beneficial to my education and quite possibly beneficial to future students I would teach. By that July, I was on a plane to the other side of the world.

KUMI NA TATU

JAPAN

After weeks of meetings and preparations, I found myself in downtown Tokyo during the summer of 2005. The purpose of the JET Program was to expose Japanese students to individuals from English speaking countries for the purpose of learning and speaking English more fluently. Participants in the JET Program were from English-speaking countries across the globe. We stayed in Tokyo's five-star Keio Plaza Hotel. We attended three-day workshops that taught us about Japanese customs, religion, foods, language, history, and other aspects of Japanese life. We also met collectively with JETs (participants) that were going to live in the same prefecture (state).

While meeting with individuals from my future prefecture, I found out I would be living in a town with one other JET named Jessica Bartkowski. Jessica was a blonde-haired, blue-eyed, Caucasian female from Vermont. Our first encounter was wonderful. This was only my second time spending an extended period of time with a person of another ethnicity, besides basic training.

DELINQUENT TO DOCTOR

My contract stated that I would be working in the small town of Yazu-Cho, Totorri for one year. Tottorri is located off the Sea of Japan, right across from South Korea. On the third day of workshops, it was time to leave Tokyo and go to our respective destinations. We all boarded buses and we were on our way to the airport. The flight from Tokyo to Tottori was less than an hour. Once Jessica and I arrived at the airport, two assistant principals and a town representative met us. We loaded into a mini van and they took us to lunch at a local eatery. As we were eating, my jet lag started setting in. After we left the restaurant, we were taken to the houses where we would live for the next twelve months.

With middle school students in Tottori, Japan.

I arrived at my temporary lodging, completely exhausted. Our host suggested that we stay with them for the first night. However, I objected to that suggestion. With all the flying and transferring from buses to cars, lugging suit cases and the fourteen hour time difference from Atlanta, I did not want to move another step. I went into my new house, briefly explored it, and I fell out on the bed at about 2:00 p.m. I was wide-awake at 3:00 a.m. I unpacked my bags and stared at the ceiling until the sun rose.

The next morning, my kocho-sensei (vice-principal) arrived at my new home and brought me a breakfast of rolls with butter in the middle, aloe yogurt, and juice. I was very happy to see him, because I had been alone for the past seventeen hours. He informed me that Jessica and I would be meeting the mayor and other figureheads that morning. He told me to be dressed in the next couple of hours and a van would be by to pick me up. Once the van arrived, Jessica was already in the back seat. When we saw each other, it was as if we were two long-lost orphaned siblings that had not seen each other in twenty years. It had been less than twenty-four hours. We instantly embraced. We had both experienced a taste of isolation and said with relief, "I am so happy to see you!"

The Japanese Exchange and Teaching Program

The next couple of weeks were devoted to becoming acclimated to my surroundings and learning my role as an Assistant Language Teacher for two middle schools and three elementary schools. My main role was to assist a bi-lingual

Japanese teacher who also spoke English with exposing Japanese students to the English language.

With elementary school students in Tottori, Japan.

After about two weeks of living in Tottori, I eventually acquired satellite television. I was provided with a television, but the only programs I was able to watch were Japanese game shows and the news. So, I had to rely on DVDs of the first two seasons of *The Family Guy* I borrowed from a fellow JET for entertainment. My internet was not working and I did not have a cell phone - pretty sad, huh?

The Exposure Theory

This was the first time in my life that I experienced a high level of isolation. I remember thinking that this must be how convicts feel in prison. I was living in a Japanese Style house surrounded by rice fields, very similar to the houses in the movie, *Crouching Tiger, Hidden Dragon.* I was experiencing a bit of homesickness, but in retrospect it was one of the best things that could have ever happened to me. When I was going through my isolation, it caused me to reflect and analyze my life on a level I had never experienced.

I was lying in bed one night, and I was trying to figure out how in the world a knucklehead from Decatur, who used to sell drugs, fight, smoke weed, break into cars, and got expelled from school, end up in Tottori, Japan teaching Japanese kids how to speak English. During this deep reflection, I had an epiphany (another traffic light moment) and simultaneously, had a vision. My vision was of a person (unidentifiable sex, race, or religion) leaping out of an open box with a broken shackle around one ankle.

While deciphering this vision, the thought of my ancestors-as-slaves came to mind. I thought about Africans in physical bondage for centuries. I also thought about mental and spiritual slavery, white supremacy, and the plethora of traps established to impede the progress of people throughout the African Diaspora. Still, I believe individuals have choices.

Present-day bondage is a result of self inflicted wounds, whether it's an unhealthy diet, breaking the law, financial irresponsibility, or lack of self-love (all personal choices). The vision I had of the person leaping out of an open box with a broken shackle represented the choice to make a positive change in life.

My Vision.

My traffic light moment was that as an adolescent, my life was a paradox. I was in advance classes; yet, I did my share of dirt and associated with individuals that displayed varied levels of delinquent behavior - selling drugs, stealing cars, gang activity, smoking weed, and fighting. But I grew up in a two-parent home, had my own room, and was provided with three-square-meals-a-

day plus snacks. Not that there is ever a justification to be delinquent, but I had no reason to display that type of behavior.

At Hiroshima Peace Memorial Park.

As I reflected on my evolution, the one question that kept nagging me was, "Why in the hell did I do all those things when I was younger?" Then all of a sudden it came to me! *The Exposure Theory* and the idea for *The Exposure Foundation* were born. When I was younger, I had a high level of positive exposure. At the same time my negative exposure slightly exceeded my positive exposure, therefore I experienced more negative outcomes than positive outcomes. Experiencing college, graduate school, military and fraternity life, and traveling the world increased my positive exposure and decreased my negative exposure, resulting in me

159

experiencing more positive outcomes. I did not know that my journey would yield such a positive change. I told myself that if I apply *The Exposure Theory* to at-risk youth in communities in the United States, it may alleviate many of the pitfalls that certain young people face as they maneuver through life. I believed *The Exposure Theory* could be applied to individuals of all age groups, sexes, ethnicities and belief systems. It was a very profound moment in my life.

After about three weeks, I eventually attained a keitai (cell phone), a vehicle, and internet service and my feelings of isolation and homesickness subsided. I became pretty functional in my daily routine of servicing five different schools. In my off time, over the next eight months, I traveled all over Japan, to cities like Osaka, Kyoto, Tokyo, Hiroshima, and even Okinawa during my off-time. I also traveled to Thailand and South Korea. My Japanese experience was great! I developed a great respect for other cultures and a greater desire to travel the world - which I continued to do once I was finished with the JET Program and returned to the states in February of 2006. I no longer drank or took drugs, so traveling the world became my addiction.

Standing in front of the Sitting Buddha in Bangkok, Thailand.

KUMI NA NNE

WORLD TRAVELER

I have traveled to approximately thirty countries on six continents. However, I have not always been an avid traveler. I did not even leave the Southeast area of the United States until I was twenty-two, when I enlisted into the Air Force. I guess you could say I got a late start. My very first international experience was to Cancun, Mexico.

In the summer of 1999, a female friend of mine named Shannon invited me to join her on a trip organized by Atlanta's V-103 radio personalities Frank Ski, Wanda Smith, and Griff. They were new to V-103 that year and planned a trip to Cancun. Shannon and I had been hanging out for a couple months and when she presented me with the idea to go, I was hesitant because international travel was a foreign idea to me. I eventually agreed to go.

Since this was before the mandatory passport requirements, we were not required to have a passport to travel to Mexico, but we did have to present a valid birth certificate. The trip package we paid for was all-inclusive, which included flight, hotel, all meals, and all alcoholic and non-alcoholic beverages. I was still drinking in 1999, so the all-inclusive package was right up my alley. While in Cancun, I went parasailing, enjoyed a booze cruise, rode a mechanical bull, hung out at the beach, and went snorkeling. My first international experience was wonderful, and I caught the proverbial travel bug.

Parasailing in Cancun, Mexico.

My second international trip did not take place until three years later in December of 2002. This was my first cruise, which was to Nassau, Bahamas. I took this trip with two of my frat brothers and some ladies of Delta Sigma Theta. Once again, another phenomenal experience! Just like Mexico, I did not need a passport, only my birth certificate. However, I was about to receive a little motivation to attain my passport.

Shortly after I returned from the Bahamas, one of my line brothers had a wedding where I met a very nice young lady named Aaliyah. We hit it off right away. She was living in Minneapolis, Minnesota at the time. Not long after we met, I found myself in Minnesota visiting her. The morning after my first night visiting, Aaliyah, her roommate, her roommate's boyfriend and I were sitting around conversing about various topics from education to politics. Aaliyah was born oversees, had gone to school oversees, and was an avid traveler. Her roommate and the boyfriend were also avid travelers. One of the topics discussed that morning was world travel and how many visa stamps were in each of our passports.

Everyone took turns sharing his or her travel experiences and the number of stamps that they had accrued. When it came to me, my response was, "I don't have a passport." Everyone looked at me like I had a horn growing out of my head. They all looked at me like, "How in the world are you a grown man without a passport?" At a very young age, I discovered that I never wanted to be "out of the know." In all situations, I wanted to make sure I could contribute to the conversation. I was caught off guard in this particular situation.

Standing in front of Big Ben in London, England.

DELINQUENT TO DOCTOR

One of the things I pride myself on is that I am able to except constructive criticism. Once a deficiency has been identified, I could put a plan into action to rectify the situation. So, I didn't get offended by how they responded to me not having a passport. However, it did cause me to question myself. Why *didn't* I have a passport? After assessing the situation, I determined that I needed to acquire my passport as soon as possible. Once I returned to Atlanta, I started researching how to apply for a passport. I found that I could take care of everything at my local post office. I went to the post office, took two passport pictures, completed the application, and paid my filing fee. Within six weeks, I had a brand new passport and I was ecstatic! I constantly dreamed about the countries I would visit and getting my first passport stamp. My first official passport stamp was from Aruba in the spring of 2005. My travels continued when I was accepted into the JET Program.

When I returned home from Japan, my excursions did not stop. I decided upon my return, I did not want to work a 9 to 5, I just wanted to travel, and that is exactly what I did. Every other weekend I was in a different country including St. Martin, Cayman Islands, Brazil, Jamaica, Dominican Republic, England, and various other countries. My most memorable and life-changing experience was visiting Dakar, Senegal.

Senegal

As an African that was stripped of my culture, language, belief system, spirit, body, and mind, I was on a continuous quest to reclaim what was stolen from me. For a long time, I had been trying to get to Africa as a part of my quest. I wanted to see where I came from. I attempted to travel to Senegal three times and was unsuccessful. Each time, the flights were either oversold, there were mechanical problems with the plane, or my personal schedule did not permit me to go. On my fourth attempt, my mother and I found ourselves in downtown Dakar. Before we left the states, I contacted a previous coworker from Newton High School that was from Senegal, Adimu Sue, to get some helpful information about our upcoming adventure. Adimu put me in contact with his uncle, Amadou. I contacted Amadou by email to let him know when we would arrive. He was very receptive and told us to call him as soon as we landed.

With Amadou in downtown Dakar.

We arrived into Dakar at about 3:30 a.m. After getting through immigration and customs, we hailed a cab and went to the Novotel Dakar Hotel, which was right on the Atlantic Ocean. Once we settled in, I called Amadou about 7:00 a.m. He said he was on his way. At about 7:20 a.m., we received a call in the room from Amadou.

"I am downstairs," He informed us. My mother and I headed downstairs immediately.

"What do you want to do?" he asked.

"Everything!" we emphatically responded.

"Let's explore the city," he suggested.

Walking down the streets of Dakar was like attending a family reunion with people I didn't know, but resembled many people that I did know. It was absolutely wonderful! After I thought about it for a moment, seeing people that looked similar to me completely made sense. According to my research, my ancestors were stolen from this part of Africa and forced into slavery. While being amongst the people of Senegal, many of the people I encountered attempted to speak to me in Wolof (the native language) and French (as a result of French Colonialism, and Imperialism). They thought I was Senegalese because of my features and I loved it!

Goree Island

My mother and I explored the city, talking with the Senegalese people, eating the food, and we purchased some local clothing and artwork. But nothing compares to the highlight of the trip, which was going to Goree Island. Goree Island is located of the coast of Senegal, the most western country on the continent of Africa and was a slave port.

Sign in front of the Slave Mansion.

While on the island, we visited *Maison Des Esclaves*, which means "House of Slaves" or "Slave Mansion" in French. *Maison Des Esclaves* is a two-level building facing the Atlantic Ocean. According to the Goree Island historian and guide, the slave overseers lived on the top floor, and the African captives were stored downstairs in separate cages. The captives were divided into males, females, and children. The conditions were deplorable! Our ancestors were crammed into small areas while having to endure the prolonged presence and stench of feces, urine, and female menstruation. Women had to suffer the added violation and indignity of rape. Imagine living and eating in these conditions for several months before boarding slave ships headed to the Americas!

Goree Island.

I had previously talked to a few people about their experience traveling to the "Mother Land." Many expressed sadness and shed tears, but also excitement. That was not my reaction. I was pissed off! I kept wondering, "What type of evil person could do such horrible things to other human beings?" At the same time I was empowered. I say *empowered* because I was standing in a place where my ancestors were kidnapped and thrown into slavery. If not Goree Island, they were taken from an environment very similar and generations later, I - their descendent - had returned. Everything had come full circle.

Standing in the center of *Maison Des Esclaves.*

There was a door on the bottom floor of the Slave Mansion that led to the Atlantic Ocean called, "The Door of No Return" appropriately named because once African captives were dragged over the threshold, they never saw their homeland again. Four centuries later I walked back through that door. This was an experience that changed my life forever.

Standing outside of "The Door of No Return."

KUMI NA TANO

STUPID PILL

After being an educator, I decided that I would not ever work a 9 to 5 job again - with the exception of teaching. I did not view teaching as a job, because it was my passion and I enjoyed helping children reach optimal levels of success. To supplement my income and create more options for myself, I decided to upgrade my realtor's license to a real estate broker's license. The purpose was to be able to have other realtors work under me and I could make a commission from their sales. I took the course and passed my brokers test successfully the first time. Many of my other classmates were not as successful. As I continued to bolster my arsenal of options, something from my past came back to bite me in the butt, really hard!!

When I use to get in trouble as an adolescent, my father use to say that "I took a stupid pill" and whenever I would go out, or leave town, he would always say, "Make sure you do not take any stupid pills." The "stupid pill" was not thinking about the negative consequences of all of your actions before you commit to something. I was doing pretty well until the "Dodge Magnum Debacle."

Dodge Magnum Debacle

About six months prior to me going to Japan, I was presented with a proposition or "favor" from a *seemingly* close friend of mine. I say seemingly, because I *thought* she was my friend, but it turned out that she was not. For the purpose of not putting her on "front street," we are going to call the person of this cautionary tale, "Leslie." Leslie called and asked me if I would co-sign with her for a car loan. I know what you're thinking! You're saying, "I know there is no way in the world that Rashad would co-sign on a car for *anybody*, because that is not financially intelligent." In all cases that would be true. Unfortunately, I made the wrong decision.

Leslie was the equivalent of a sister to me. We had known each other since we were children and our families knew each other very well. In addition, Leslie came into a large sum of money (in the millions) as a result of a civil law suit. She helped me out with rent, food, or just spending money, during my college years. When I was preparing for law school, she even paid for me to attend Kaplan, which was a school that prepared me to take the Law School Admission Test (LSAT). I believed I was indebted to her. And yes, I thought about going to law school briefly. Let's move on.

STUPID PILL 🦂

Leslie called me to co-sign on a Dodge Magnum. Her pitch to me was that her current car was not reliable, and she needed a vehicle immediately for the purpose of transporting children that she had custody of. I know what you're asking: If she had millions, why couldn't she purchase a car herself, in cash? I asked that same exact question. Her reply was that her money was tied up in investments, stocks, and bonds. She promised me that the car would be paid off within a few months. She also offered me $2000 for my troubles.

I usually make logical decisions, utilizing my brain, versus my heart and emotions. My mistake was making a decision with my emotions, feeling indebted, and allowing money to be my motivation. Ultimately, I signed the dotted line and took a check for $2000. It sounded like a good deal at the time. Boy was I wrong! This decision ignited a series of negative events.

It turns out that Leslie was not as financially stable as I thought she was. Over the next few months, she did pay the car note on time. When I departed for Japan, the payments were still coming, but they were not on time, arriving one or two days late. Eventually one or two days, turned to weeks, and then to months. I came back from Japan a little earlier than I had planned. Before, I left for Japan, I was forced to tell my parents about the bone-headed decision I had made, because I needed them to monitor the situation. Since the situation was getting progressively worse, I did not want to burden them any longer.

175

Once I returned home, there were no payments being made, period. Leslie informed me that due to some bad business deals, most of her money was depleted. I pleaded with her to sign the car over to me, so that I could trade the car in for a cheaper car. Even though the car loan would be upside down, I could still keep my credit in tact. My credit score was 807 and I wanted to maintain that status. She refused to give the car up. As my grandmother use to say, "I was 38 hot," but there was nothing I could do.

I had creditors calling me, asking me for payment. I was receiving parking tickets in the mail because she was illegally parking the car, but the registration was in my name. I was catching much grief for a car that I had never driven. One day I received a phone call from a repossession company. They called to inform me that they had repossessed the Dodge Magnum and I needed to come collect the possessions that were left in the car. I went to claim the contents left in the car and find out what the next phase of this bad dream was. I was instructed to talk to the finance company that held the car note.

I called the finance company the next day and they informed me that the car would be auctioned off to the highest bidder to satisfy the balance of what was owed. Additionally, if the car was not auctioned off for the full balance of the car note, I would be responsible for the balance. About two weeks later, I received some good news and some bad news. The good news was that the car was sold at auction. The bad news was that I was solely responsible for a balance of approximately $15,000 and they wanted their money - immediately.

To sort out my situation, I sat down to have a conversation with my parents. I didn't have the money to pay the debt, nor did I want to have any blemishes on my credit report, which would cause my credit score to decline. My mother empathized with me and said she would have done the same thing in my position because of the relationship I thought I had with Leslie. My father suggested that if all my options were exhausted, he would borrow the money against his mortgage to assist me with my dilemma. I was deeply moved by this gesture. I told him that I would pay back the loan as soon as possible, because I absolutely hate owing anyone anything at anytime including - my parents.

My immediate problem was resolved; however, I was in the red as a result. It was a very stressful time in my life. "Not to worry," I repeated to myself, "in order to discern when a greater power is talking to you, you must sit still and pay attention." In the midst of orchestrating damage control I was introduced to two grand opportunities: rejoining the work force and going back to school.

KUMI NA SITA

DR. ROSEMOND

Before I knew the outcome of my car situation, my mother informed me that her school had a business education position open. At the time, I was traveling and I was not interested in working at all. As I started receiving statements in the mail to satisfy my debt, I started to reconsider my position on reentering the workforce. During my time of reflection, my mother informed me that the position was still available. Once again, I had a traffic light moment. My inner voice told me that this opportunity came right on time. So I started working at Marcus Garvey Middle School in December of 2006. I had also enrolled at Argosy University Atlanta to pursue a Doctorate in Education four months prior to going to work.

Before leaving for Japan, two female colleagues who had recently become doctors suggested that I pursue my doctorate in education. Before entering education, I had never thought of pursuing a doctorate degree. I thought I was finished with school; obviously I was not. I made preparations before leaving the states so that I could start school as soon as I returned home. Within a few months of returning from Japan, I was working as a full-time teacher, and I was a full-time student. Over the next few months, I settled into my new position as a business education middle school teacher and a doctoral student. I was also able to pay my father back in full over a period of eight months. I enjoyed my new teaching position and my journey towards becoming Dr. Rosemond.

Pursuing a doctorate in Curriculum and Instruction was not an easy journey. As I maneuvered through the process I began to understand that it was not supposed to be easy - if it was, everyone would have one. There were six major phases that I had to go through before reaching graduation day: course work; successfully completing a comprehensive exam; writing chapters one through three and completing a proposal defense; qualifying for Institutional Review Board (IRB) and district approval; actually conducting the study; and then writing chapters four and five of a dissertation and completing a final defense successfully.

Course Work

The course work consisted of forty-eight semester credit hours and twelve credit hours of dissertation requirements. Core requirements consisted of classes about education, curriculum, academic research, and statistics. These classes assisted me with becoming a better educator, researcher and writer. My most challenging class was *Program Evaluation Methods*, which was taught by the campus president, Dr. Sheldon. Dr. Sheldon was known as one of the hardest professors, if not *the* hardest professor in the program. I chose to take his class because I believed if I could survive his class, I could make it through anything. As I projected, the class was very challenging and I came very close to failing the class with a grade of C, because I could not earn lower than a B on the graduate level.

At the time, I was working as a full-time teacher and I called Dr. Sheldon and I asked if I could come by and meet with him. He told me to come by. I told one of my fellow teachers to cover my class and left work in the middle of the day and went on campus to talk with him. We talked for about two hours on subjects consisting of education, politics, and world affairs. The two most important things he said to me were: 1. Individuals that are pursuing a Doctorate just for a pay raise are going to have a more challenging journey than those that are pursing an education and 2. Everyone that starts a doctoral program will not finish, because everyone can not write a dissertation. He told me that I displayed the ability to complete a doctoral program, and with that being said he gave me a chance to improve an assignment he believed that I should have done better on. I made the improvements that he suggested and ultimately passed the class successfully, which allowed me to continue on my academic journey. If I had to retake that class, it would have set me back one year behind my projected graduation date.

Comprehensive Examination

After completing my course work, I had to complete the comprehensive exam or "comps." The exam consisted of five questions that had to be answered in essay form. Each response had to be between five to ten pages per question. Basically, I had to write a miniature dissertation. The university gave us seven days to complete the exam. We were advised to utilize our textbooks, and current peered reviewed articles. I worked on my comps everyday for seven days from sun up to sun down. Once I finished my exam, I had a total of forty-five pages. I successfully passed my comprehensive exam and was granted eligibility to begin my dissertation courses.

I completed my comprehensive exam, chose a dissertation topic, and completed the first three chapters of my dissertation while taking my *Writing for Research* class in the summer of 2008. The title of my dissertation was, "The Effectiveness of a Truancy Intervention System on Middle Grade Students." There are five chapters in a dissertation and my *Writing for Research* professor, Dr. Barbara Holmes' belief was that all her students would complete chapters one to three and a PowerPoint in preparation for their proposal defense. Dr. Holmes also became my dissertation chair.

Proposal Defense

Dr. Holmes created a doctoral cohort model which was formed to ensure that doctoral students assist each other during the doctoral process. We all had areas of the process that we were proficient in, and in the areas where we were deficient, we helped each other. After completing *Writing for Research*, I enrolled into *Dissertation I* and continued to refine the first three chapters of my dissertation in preparation for my proposal defense. A proposal defense is where doctoral candidates present their study to their dissertation committee for the purpose of being granted permission to execute study. After working diligently through *Dissertation I* and *II*, I passed my proposal defense on February 5, 2009. Now I was ready to conduct my study, but I had two more hurdles in front of me - IRB and district approval.

IRB & District Approval

I conducted my study at Marcus Garvey Middle School in Turner County. Before I could conduct the study, I had to acquire district permission first, as well as permission from Argosy University. The purpose of approval from both bodies was to basically make sure that any study that was conducted was safe and ethical for all people involved. I received permission from both bodies by the end of the summer of 2008. I started conducting my study of truancy intervention in the fall of 2008.

The Study

As I previously stated, I conducted a study on the effectiveness of a truancy intervention system on middle grade students. Marcus Garvey Middle School had a truancy intervention plan in place for about two years, but the effectiveness had not been measured. I was in right place at the right time. I conducted an embedded triangulation mixed-method study (I used three types of data).

Archival data were used in a mixed-methods study to examine the effectiveness of a truancy intervention system at an urban middle school and its effect on students' behavior, academic performance, and attendance. Factors contributing to the patterns of truancy were explored by triangulating data from interviews, observations, and a document review. The number of discipline referrals increased from before the system was implemented to one year later. The grade point average of the children decreased in the same period. However, the number of unexcused absences decreased. Analysis of the interviews and observations found three factors contributing to truancy at the school. The factors consisted of family and parental, community, and personal. Recommendations for further research included exploring the relationships between social bonds, truancy, and truancy intervention.

Final Defense

I completed my study and finished chapters four and five. I completed the final slides of my PowerPoint for my final defense and I also sent my entire paper to an editor for my final edit. According to the rules and regulations, my dissertation had to be perfect before it went to the editor for review. I was scheduled to defend my dissertation on August 26, 2009 at 5:00 p.m.

DELINQUENT TO DOCTOR

The day before I was supposed to defend I caught a cold. I was sick, figuratively and literally. The night before my final defense I consumed a lot of over-the-counter medications, including Theraflu, Nyquil, and Benedryl. I was not going to miss my defense for anything in the world. The next day I felt much better and I reported to the school an hour before it was time for me to defend. I wanted to make sure that my PowerPoint was set up and ready to go. Once 5:00 p.m. came, it was show time and I started my presentation. By 5:26 p.m., my presentation was done, and now it was time for any individuals that were at my defense to ask questions. I was so concise and definitive that not one person had a question. After three years of a grueling process, Dr. Holmes announced, "I now present Dr. Rosemond." Dr. Holmes and I embraced and I felt like a huge weight was lifted off my shoulders.

I had reached another major milestone in my life, and just like past milestones, once I reached a certain goal I always experienced a high level of reflection. While I was working on my doctorate, I was cultivating *The Exposure Foundation* vision. It was my passion, and something I very much wanted to do. I was also teaching, something I enjoyed, even though I did not enjoy the bureaucracy of the public school system. A year prior to attaining my doctorate, I knew I had reached my breaking point and it was time to leave the teaching profession, but I stayed one more year to stack some money - doing the responsible thing.

With my parents at the Argosy Graduation.

Retirement

I was at a point in my life where I was able to do what I wanted to do, when I wanted to do it, and how I wanted to do it. For the first time in my life I felt 98% free, and the only reason why it was not 100% is because I do not have any control over what a greater power (Allah, Ya, Ja, God, Jehovah, I AM) has planned for me. I believed that if I had to get up everyday and do something, it would be because I *wanted* to do it, not because I *had* to do it.

At age thirty-two, the Creator had allowed me to be in a position to help people without asking for compensation and without *having* to have an income. Retirement is usually for individuals in their mid '60s. Since retiring, I have been often

185

asked how I retired at such a young age. I reply, "Number one, I do not allow money to be my motivation, and number two, I live below my means." Third, I tell a story about how I learn from all aspects of life, including nature. The story I tell is of how I even learn from a squirrel preparing for a long winter.

Before a long winter, squirrels collect as many acorns as possible and store them in their drey (nest). They store enough food to sustain them for the long winter months. I've done something very similar. Figuratively speaking, for the past twenty years I have collected ten acorns per day, but only consumed two acorns and stored eight. I find that the average person collects ten acorns per day and consumes twelve acorns, leaving them in the red two acorns per day, which causes them to live beyond their means. This behavior causes individuals to do things they do not necessarily want to do for money, to meet their financial responsibilities.

My mother told me that my grandfather used to have a saying that he always lived by. It went like this: "Live your life in a way, that you can tell anybody to go to hell, on any given day," and that's what I started doing. I decided that was going to be my last year teaching in the public system and I was going to retire and devote my life to philanthropic work and *The Exposure Foundation*. In the midst of my retirement and running the operations of *The Exposure Foundation* fulltime, I received an opportunity that I could not refuse.

KUMI NA SABA

TANZANIA

By the spring of 2009, I had done some extensive traveling. I had seen the statue of Yeshua in Rio de Janeiro, Brazil, experienced most of the islands in the Caribbean, visited the Stone Henge formations in England, and gone scuba diving in Sydney, Australia. I've waded in underground streams in Phukett, Thailand and walked through the slave dungeons of Goree Island, Senegal, and Cape Coast, Ghana. Even still, I was about to be faced with an opportunity that would trump all my previous experiences.

During the last semester of my teaching career, I received an email from a colleague who worked in a neighboring school district, informing me of an opportunity of travel to Tanzania for five weeks. Of course, my initial response was, "When do we leave?" But I had to figure out what this entire excursion entailed.

According to the information, a former professor, Dr. Fredoline Anunobi of The Center for International and African studies of the American Institution for Resource and Human Development (AIRHD) recently received a grant from the Fulbright-Hays Group Projects Abroad Program. The purpose of the grant was to take a group of local teachers to Tanzania for five weeks of global exposure. Dr. Anunobi stated that all individuals that were interested should forward a current resume, a typed explanation of why they should be considered for this opportunity, a copy of their passport, and a check for $923. He further stated that if we were not chosen, the money would be refunded.

At first glance, I was somewhat skeptical. Yes, I was very interested, but in this day and age of sophisticated scams, I was not looking to be hustled. I proceeded to satisfy all the application requirements. However, instead of forwarding my information, I decided to contact Dr. Anunobi by phone and request a face-to-face meet and greet. Once we made contact with each other, he agreed to meet with me the next evening after I was finished with my school day. After getting off the phone with Dr. Anunobi I forwarded him my curricular vitae, philosophy of education, and references.

After school the next day, I proceeded to Dr. Anunobi's house. I did not know what to expect and I was somewhat nervous. When I met Dr. Anunobi, we connected immediately. We were definitely kindred spirits. He invited me in and we discussed our backgrounds and he also explained what the Fulbright Scholarship entailed. He told me that there was an evaluation process for accepting teachers, but he was so impressed with my background that I was accepted immediately. He informed me that there would be a pre-departure meeting within two months, and then we would be on our way to Dar Es Salaam, Tanzania for five weeks. I felt like I was on top of the world and I was ready to go.

Two months later, I attended the pre-departure briefing and met the other teachers that were going on the five week excursion to Tanzania. Dr. Anunobi and I left three days early, before everyone else to finalize housing arrangements and transportation. En route to Dar Es Salaam, we had a brief layover in Amsterdam. Unfortunately, there was a thunderstorm the night we were supposed to leave the States and we did not leave Atlanta until three hours after our designated time of departure. Hence, we missed our connection flight in Amsterdam.

I was bothered, but at the same time the situation gave me a chance to explore Amsterdam and the "Red Light District." After I made sure Dr. Anunobi was settled in the hotel room, I ventured out to see what I could see. I had always heard that the Red Light District was a place that was uncensored. This is a place where EVERYTHING was legal from marijuana consumption to prostitution. No, I was not going to the Red Light District to participate in any seedy activities! I was just going to see what all the hoopla was about.

Whenever I travel, I always research the local public transportation. I've navigated my way through Bangkok on a tuk-tuk and on the Shinkansen (Bullet Train) in Japan. Lucky for me, there was a pretty sophisticated rail system in Amsterdam. I also made sure I had a map of the area and the locations that I wanted to visit and experience. I was able to find my way to the Red Light District pretty quickly and took the train directly from the airport in less than forty-five minutes.

A Coffee Shop that allows the consumption of cannabis in the Red Light District.

Once I got to the area, I noticed a lot of stores selling pornographic paraphernalia. There were establishments that advertised live nude shows, and people were smoking weed everywhere, like they were smoking cigarettes. My overall opinion was that the Red Light District was overrated and I was not impressed. I was there less than forty-five minutes and I was out. I returned to the hotel and went to sleep with thoughts of Tanzania on my mind.

The next day we boarded our plane successfully and we were on our way. We had a brief layover in Nairobi, Kenya for about three hours. We caught a small plane for the last leg of our trip and arrived at Dar Es Salaam International Airport in the middle of the night. We went to our lodging, which was a dorm at a Catholic School. The next morning we woke up and finalized our lodging and transportation for the next five weeks. Later on that night, we met the rest of the group at the airport. The next five weeks were a series of life changing experiences.

Meeting with students at an elementary school in Dar Es Salaam.

Our purpose for this trip was to become exposed to life in Africa, and Tanzania in particular, so as educators, we could tell people first hand about life in that part of the world. We attended seminars at the University of Dar Es Salaam on Tanzanian history, local belief systems, language, culture and customs, topography and geography, government, natural resources, wildlife and tourism, agriculture, and the post-economic reform period. We also visited and explored five major areas - Dar Es Salaam, Bagamoyo, the island of Zanzibar, Arusha, and Kilimanjaro.

Standing in the slave memorial in Zanzibar.

The seminars were very informative. There were three things that really stood out for me. First, before I visited Tanzania, I was under the impression that Africans were all Muslims before being enslaved and indoctrinated with Christianity by Europeans. I was wrong. Apparently, the Arabs were doing the same thing on the east coast of Africa, that the Europeans were doing on the west coast, which was using religion as a tool to enslave Africans. The Europeans used Christianity and the Arabs used Islam. I learned that Africans throughout the continent had a belief system that predated both religions.

Next, a few of us in the group were trying to figure out why the largest lake in the region was called "Lake Victoria," because Victoria was from England. We found out that the lake was named "Victoria Lake" by an explorer named David Livingston. He was the first European to travel to that part of Africa and see the massive lake. He took it upon himself to name the lake after the queen of England. We all understood the story, but we could not understand why Tanzania, now independent, still referred to the lake as "Lake Victoria." When asked, the Tanzanians seemed a bit confused and replied that it had always been that way. After talking to some of the other professors and researching, we found the true name of the lake is Lake Nyanza. Europeans had a tendency of renaming people, places, land masses and bodies of water in attempts to rewrite history and glorify themselves.

The third thing I discovered through these seminars related to Tanzania's natural resources, which proved to be the most interesting and alarming. Our presenter explained to us that the majority of Tanzanians lived in poverty - A family of four lives on the equivalent of one US dollar per day. The presenter also explained to us that Tanzania had many different natural resources including oil, rubber, and Tanzanite. We wondered why Tanzanians were not financially benefiting when the country is rich with so many valuable resources. The professor explained that the citizens of Tanzania only receives 3% of the profits produced by the natural resources of Tanzania, and Western Corporations profit from the other 97%. We were pissed! It was also confirmed that the intentional "Underdevelopment of Africa" was prevalent throughout the continent. It is clearly outlined and explained in Walter Rodney's, *How Europe Underdeveloped Africa*.

Over the next five weeks I explored Dar Es Salaam and enjoyed the food, shopping and the beaches. In Bagamoyo, I explored slave dungeons and castles. The entire island of Zanzibar was a major Arab slave port. We even stayed in an old hotel that used to be a slave dungeon. I also had a chance to go scuba diving off the coast of Zanzibar in the form of a sunken ship dive. We traveled thirteen hours from Dar Es Salaam to Arusha and Kilimanjaro. We were supposed to climb Mt. Kilimanjaro, but time did not permit. However, we were able to experience a real African safari at the Arusha National Park. Upon returning from Arusha, we prepared to return to the States three days later.

My trip to Tanzania was exciting, as well as educational. I learned three lessons as a result of my experience: 1. My daily problems are trivial. I don't have problems; I have challenges compared to what my ancestors went through - how dare I complain! 2. I owe a great debt to the people that came before me. 3. In order for me to be a true humanitarian and philanthropist who helps others, regardless of the situation, their background, and belief system, I must continue to examine myself. I need to ensure that my deficiencies are addressed and constantly strive for optimal levels of success. I called this process a "self-audit." These lessons provided me the additional tools I needed to further the vision of *The Exposure Foundation* once I returned to Atlanta.

KUMI NA NANE

EXPOSURE

The Exposure Theory was born in Tottori, Japan. My frustrations with the bureaucracy in the public school system was the catalyst for establishing my non-profit, *The Exposure Foundation.* I don't believe today's public school system is really set up to help kids on an optimal level. I have always told my students that there are two types of teachers, those that care about students and paycheck teachers. I explained to them that I genuinely cared and my purpose as an educator was to keep the brothers out of prison and the females off of the stripper pole, figuratively and literally. I believed that the combination of unmotivated children, uninvolved parents and a public school system that seemed to be more concerned with statistics than the total growth of the child was a recipe for disaster. I believed I should be doing more. Consequently, *The Exposure Foundation* became a reality.

In the beginning, I had no clue on how to start a non-profit organization. However, my father has always told me not to re-invent the wheel, simply learn from others that have already established similar organizations. That's exactly what I did. Between 2006 and 2007, I settled on a name, created a logo, registered with the Georgia Secretary of State, established an EIN, gained 501(c)3 status, opened a bank account, created a website, printed business cards, and attained a credit card designated solely for operations related to *The Exposure Foundation.*

Original drawing of *The Exposure Foundation* logo.

With all my paperwork in order, I believed I was ready for business. I had one problem: I did not have any money. However, I did have a great vision; I just don't think I realized how great the vision was. One of my mentors informed me that if I was waiting for a certain amount of money to materialize before I decided to help people, I would never start. That really hit home. So, I did not wait for grants and donations. I decided that people who look like me should have the opportunity to experience all aspects of what life has to offer and began to put things in action.

In my opinion, there are many types of organizations that claim to help or mentor children, but they seem very limited in their scope. You can't just take kids to the movies, bowling, or on other activities, feed them cake and fruit punch, and send them on their way. I also think that many children are solely involved in sports. These activities are cool, but insufficient. Most children are already used to sports and related activities. My charge was to create a paradigm shift to create positive change. That change began on the Ocoee River in the Blue Ridge Mountains of Tennessee.

I had previously gone rafting twice and noticed there were very little people of color (I was actually the only African on one trip). This really bothered me! I found that when I participated in related activities or traveled internationally, my experiences were similar. I wanted *The Exposure Foundation* to be known for offering alternative trips and also set it apart from other non-profits geared toward helping children in the community.

The Exposure Foundation's first self-discovery outing was rafting. I had one female participant, one male participant, and one female chaperone. My chaperone was very exposed to various activities and world travel. Both children had very limited exposure outside of their communities. The kids were nervous initially, but after they came down the river, they were ready to go again. That day it was confirmed that community service and philanthropic work was my mission in life.

Rafting on the Ocoee River.

Through my experiences as Executive Director of *The Exposure Foundation*, I have discovered that community service should not be limited to a couple days out of the year or around some holiday. Community service should be carried out 365 days of the year. Giving someone a turkey or feeding the homeless on Christmas and Thanksgiving is very thoughtful, but the needy were hungry the day before and they are going to be hungry the day after. Much of my philanthropic work is based on an old Chinese proverb, "Give a man a fish and he will eat for a day. Teach him how to fish and he will eat for a lifetime." That is why the vision of positive exposure is invaluable for individuals to be successful in life. *The Exposure Foundation* is a culmination of my life up to this point. For me, *The Exposure Foundation* is not a job or just a program, it is a lifestyle.

The Official Logo of *The Exposure Foundation*.

Mission

The mission of the foundation is to improve the quality of life for youth and families. *The Exposure Foundation* exposes individuals to ideas and experiences outside of their immediate belief system and physical environment, addressing their immediate deficiencies, and assisting them with achieving optimal levels of success. The mission is also accomplished by providing youth and families some of the essential tools and skills necessary for building character, increasing self-esteem and self-confidence, meeting positive friends, developing strong academic skills, and making informed choices. Early intervention will significantly decrease aberrant behavior such as gang related activity, involvement with drugs, dropping out of school, early sexual activity, and the risk of incarceration. Special emphasis is placed on "at risk" youth and their families. Services are designed for youth ages eight to eighteen.

Exposure Foundation students at the Atlanta Motor Speedway.

I started building *The Exposure Foundation*, had a full-time teaching position, and pursued my doctorate in the latter half of

2006. In the first three years of the organization's existence, I could only devote partial time to the program. In the past year, I have devoted all of my time to the success of "Exposing Youth to the World." Getting people out of their comfort zone (the box) is challenging, but necessary. With the assistance of my devoted volunteers, we have been able to facilitate a myriad of workshops, community service projects, and self-discovery outings.

We conduct health, diet, fitness, financial literacy, and conflict resolution workshops. Community service projects involving both students and their parents consist of picking up trash from our adopted road and feeding the homeless. Our self-discovery outings are varied; we've gone zip-lining, camping, horseback riding, taken an airplane ride, a helicopter ride, visited the NASA Space Center, rode in race cars at the Atlanta Motor Speedway (Richard Petty Experience), and attended a hockey match.

The Exposure Foundation also implements a healthy diet during all workshops and activities. Children are not allowed to eat any junk food. No cheese burgers, fried chicken, Hot Cheetos, candy, sodas, pork products, or fried foods can be consumed at anytime. Instead, we eat turkey sandwiches on wheat bread, granola bars, fruit, vegetables and water. Of course, a great number of the participants have reservations about the menu, initially. In the end they enjoy the meal and snacks we provide for them (They have no choice).

EXPOSURE

Each child is also responsible for learning the *Exposure Creed* and has to recite it on request. I was inspired to write the *Exposure Creed* about five years ago while cycling. I am not sure where the inspiration came from. I have only written two pieces of literature in my life, *Being Pimped* and the *Exposure Creed*. As I was riding my bike, I thought, "It's impossible for me to grow if I live in the box." I went directly home, because I felt compelled to put words to paper. The first thing I could put my hands on were a pen, and some yellow post-it notes. Within about fifteen minutes, the *Exposure Creed* was born.

Exposure Creed

It's impossible for me to grow if I live in a box.
I will discard inferior thoughts, failure, a defeated mentality,
mediocrity and complacency.
I will embrace excellence, a positive attitude,
community service and victory.
I am a walking example of inspiration.
I have chosen to live, not just exist.
-Dr. Abdalla Rashad Tau

The *Exposure Creed* embodies all the elements needed for participants to adopt in order to attain their personal endeavors as they maneuver through the numerous programs *The Exposure Foundation* offers. Approximately 200 children and adults have been exposed to things outside of their immediate belief system and environment, in and around the Atlanta area. My vision is to collaborate with similar programs and expand on a statewide, countrywide, and international level. The *Exposure Theory* has not only helped the participants to evolve, exposure has also continued to help me evolve as well.

Zip Lining.

A helicopter ride.

KUMI NA TISA

TAU

My evolution is constant. Recently, I changed my name. This was not a decision that I took lightly. Changing my name was the conclusion to a journey that began in 1987. That year, I was ten years old and in the 5th grade at Canby Lane Elementary School. Little did I know that I would be exposed to a concept that would impact me twenty-four years later.

Slave Name

During my 5th grade year, I had a classmate named Jeff Reed. After coming back from one of our holiday breaks, I noticed that Jeff had a new name. His name was no longer Jeff Reed, it was Oluwa Mangaliso. Of course being the immature, ignorant child that I was at the time, I thought his name change was extremely funny, as did the rest of my classmates.

One day, our regular teacher was out sick and we had a substitute teacher. I remember the substitute as a black male with a medium build, wearing a three piece brown suit with a bow tie. He introduced himself as Mr. Rasheed, and then took attendance. For those of you that do not remember the substitute teacher taking attendance, almost all of them used to have trouble pronouncing unfamiliar or foreign names. So, of course the whole class was anticipating Mr. Rasheed saying Oluwa's name, so that we could get a good laugh. All of sudden he said and mispronounced his name, and the whole class busted out laughing. Mr. Rasheed looked around and did not react at all. He simply looked at Oluwa and said, "Don't worry Oluwa. They're just mad because they have slave names and we don't." I remember the entire class being upset and proclaiming, "I ain't no slave! I ain't no slave!" We were all pretty upset about Mr. Rasheed's comment.

Mind, Body, & Spiritual Control

Eight years later, I was sitting in an African history class at Benedict College. Our professor was discussing the European Triangle Slave Trade and slavery in America. He explained that Africans needed to be controlled once they reached their designated plantations. The professor emphasized that control was achieved by forcing slaves to speak a European language, practice Christianity, wear European clothes, and take on a European first name, as well as the last name of the slave owner. Their meaningful African names were replaced with new slave names. All of sudden I had a traffic light moment and I flashbacked to that day in class with Mr. Rasheed. I finally understood what Mr. Rasheed was talking about. I realized that *I* had a slave name! I was not prepared to change my name at that point, however the seed was planted.

TAU

Roots

That proverbial seed started to sprout in my early twenties. In 1977, the week-long miniseries *Roots* aired on national TV. It was based on the family lineage of the Pulitzer Prize recipient, Alex Haley. Mr. Haley wrote *Roots* after tracing his family roots back to the Gambia in West Africa. The movie chronicles the life of his ancestor, Kunta Kinte, who was kidnapped from West Africa and enslaved in America in 1767. I believed I watched certain parts of the miniseries earlier in my life, but I had not watched it in its entirety. When I was about twenty-five, I decided to take a day and watch the whole miniseries. There was one very profound scene in the movie that caused my name change seed to start sprouting.

Kunta Kinte was very rebellious and did not want to have anything to do with being a slave. He made all attempts to escape every chance that he got. In one particular scene, Kunta made an attempt to escape and was captured by the plantation overseer. The plantation overseer brought Kunta back to the plantation and tied him to a pole, and stripped off his shirt. The overseer was attempting to break Kunta out of his rebellious ways. The overseer always felt that Kunta was going to be a problem because he was African born and not born into slavery. The overseer instructed another slave to whip Kunta with a leather whip. The goal of the whipping was for Kunta to stop referring to himself as Kunta Kinte, and start calling himself Toby. He also made sure all the other slaves on the plantation were witnesses to Kunta's whipping.

This was a way of implementing a slave mentality in order to control the slaves.

The overseer told Kunta Kinte that his new name was Toby and he was going to whip him until he learned his new name. He also told him that when his master gave him something, he should take it, because it was good.

"What's your name?" the overseer asked after ordering that first lash.

"Kunta, Kunta Kinte."

"No, your name is Toby," insisted the overseer.

"What's your name?" after striking Kunta with another blow.

"Kunta Kinte."

The overseer continued to order the whipping of Kunta, and Kunta refused to say his new name. After being whipped over and over and again, Kunta finally conceded. The whip was thrown one last time and the overseer asked, "What is your name?"

Kunta, dejected, answered, "Toby."

"That's a good nigger, cut him down," he finally said after making Kunta repeat Toby two more times.

At that point, I was convinced I was going to change my name!

Embracing Toby

There was a point in history when we were beaten, raped, and lynched for not disowning our culture! Today, we disown our true selves willingly and unknowingly. I call this condition "The

TAU

Embracing Toby Syndrome." We don't have to be beaten into being Toby anymore; we embrace being Toby, figuratively speaking. For example, most Africans in America and throughout the Diaspora practice the religion of our oppressors, Christianity. We celebrate European Holidays, and of course, we give our children European names. What if most Japanese parents gave their children Mexican names? Would that make sense? Most people find my example hilarious, but Africans with European names have become normal. It has been explained to me that African names present a challenge when children grow up and begin seeking employment. Some Black parents believe an African name on a resume turns away prospective employers. That logic is fatally flawed! (Can you say President Barack Hussein Obama? Oh! Ok!)

Famous Name Changes

In the process of changing my name, I started thinking about all of the influential Africans that have changed their names. The people that came to mind were: Kwame Ture (Stokely Carmichael), Muhammad Ali (Cassius Marcellus Clay, Jr.), Louis Farrakhan Muhammad (Louis Eugene Walcott), Jamil Abdullah Al-Amin (Hubert Gerold Brown), El Hajj Malik El-Shabazz (Malcolm Little), Mutulu Shakur (Jeral Wayne Williams), Geronimo Ji Jaga (Elmer Pratt), Ahmad Rashad (Robert Earl Moore), Elijah Muhammad (Elijah Robert Poole), Kareem Abdul-Jabbar (Ferdinand Lewis Alcindor, Jr.) and countless others. I

209

started reading their biographies to examine their life paths and reasons for changing their names. The common thread I found was a high sense of freedom gained after discarding a way of thinking. They believed they were previously indoctrinated and had embraced a new belief system that enhanced their lives. The act of dropping their slave names was a major component of their maturation process. I definitely wanted that sense of freedom and believed dropping my slave name would be part of me getting back what was stolen from my ancestors on the plantation.

Before I began my name search, I wanted to know the origin and meaning of my immediate name. According to my research, Mack is Gaelic or Scottish for "son of," Rashad is Swahili for "righteousness, and good judgment and counsel" and Rosemond is German for "horse protector." I knew my name in its entirety did not fit me. For the past ten years I have flirted with different names that I thought would be right for me, but nothing really felt right. The one name that I entertained was Rashad Ali El-Shabazz. Ali is Arabic for "noble, elevated, exalted, and sublime." El is Arabic for "God", and Shabazz is Arabic for "nobility and royalty." This name has origins in the Muslim faith.

Before going to Tanzania I thought I should have a Muslim name, because I thought all Africans were Muslims pre-colonialism and pre-slave trade. I was mistaken, so I decided to find a name with an African origin, not necessarily a religious affiliation. My research encompassed reading books of African names and actually talking to people that had changed their names. These individuals advised me to take my time and avoid choosing a random name. They told me to let the names that represent who I am choose me, and that is precisely what I did.

I was happy that I could keep at least one of my names, because Rashad is African. As I researched other names, I bounced ideas off of friends and relatives. I even created a chart for first, middle, and last names with their origins and meanings. I searched for names that I believed embodied who I am. I looked for names with African meanings related to being a teacher, servant of people, leader, extraordinary, and counselor.

The names I found were Tau (lion), Rashidi (thinker and counselor), Abdalla (servant of GOD), Kamau (silent warrior), and Imamu, which means "spiritual leader." All these names sounded great to me, but *Abdalla* and *Tau* chose me and they really stood out. Originally, I chose to make Rashad my first name, which would have read: *Rashad Abdalla Tau*. I liked how it read, but my initials read r-a-t. A rat is usually associated with a person who betrays a friend. I thought, "Wait a minute, that's not going to work." So I simply flipped the first and middle name to Abdalla Rashad Tau which changed my initials to A-R-T. Art is associated with the use of skill and creativity especially in the making of things that are beautiful to view, hear, or read. It was meant to be.

Abdalla Rashad Tau means "a servant of GOD, who is righteous with good counsel and judgment," and "lion," which symbolizes courage, power, royalty, dignity, authority, dominion, justice, wisdom, and ferocity. I am thankful that I was able to find my inner gift of philanthropy and community service early in my life. With my new name, I have a lot to live up to. My name denotes who I am, my God given inner gifts, my life journey, and my purpose. I will continue to sacrifice my life to help others, no matter their background, and live a life that promotes positive change. Hopefully when I leave this world, it will be a better place than I found it.

Dr. Abdalla Rashad Tau.

ISHIRINI

FINAL THOUGHTS

Delinquent to Doctor is a metaphor for change. It discusses my evolution from being non-progressive and simply existing to progressive and conscious. Obviously, I have not always made the right decisions. Still, I pride myself on learning from my mistakes, as well as others' mistakes to minimize my potential pitfalls. With all my accomplishments, I have also had some failures. My failures have made me stronger. This concept is reflected in one of my favorite quotes by Frederick Douglass which states, "Without struggle, there is no progress."

What has helped me most in life is my faith. I did not necessarily know what was at the end of each path that I ventured down, but I was not afraid of the unknown. Stepping outside of my comfort zone (the box) has allowed me to continually evolve in a positive direction. Also, I never allowed myself to except anything at face value, without researching the information for myself. I encourage others to do this as well. Even if I did not experience great success, I learned great lessons. If you find yourself stagnate or standing still and you want more out of life, you have to pick a path and move. If you don't, time will pass you by and you will be filled with countless regrets.

Being happy or miserable is a personal decision. You can do whatever you want to do in life, as long as you realize that you will have to sacrifice. I chose to make the bulk of my sacrifices early in life and reap the benefits later. It was not easy, but it was necessary so that I would not have to live in a state of mediocrity and complacency.

My message is not that you have to become a doctor to be successful in life. That was my path. My message is: If you want to have a certain quality of life, make all attempts to achieve a position more on the doctor end of the spectrum than the delinquent end. Become more of a producer and less of a consumer in society. I don't believe anyone's life is predestined. I do believe your life has infinite possibilities contingent on the choices you make. Your unconstructive past or present does not necessarily denote a negative future. You can make a change in your life at any time. Just like the rest of my autobiography, your life has yet to be written in its entirety. It's your choice to be ordinary or extraordinary.

NEVER LET ME DOWN

We are all here for a reason on a particular path
You don't need a curriculum to know that you are part of the math
Cats think I'm delirious, but I'm so damn serious
That's why I expose my soul to the globe, the world
I'm trying to make it better for these little boys and girls
I'm not just another individual, my spirit is a part of this
That's why I get spiritual, but I get my hymns from Him
So it's not me, it's He that's lyrical
I'm not a miracle, I'm a heaven-sent instrument
My rhythmatic regimen navigates melodic notes for your soul and your
mental
That's why I'm instrumental
Vibrations is what I'm into
Yeah, I need my loot by rent day
But that is not what gives me the heart of Kunte Kinte
I'm trying give us "us free" like Cinque
I can't stop, that's why I'm hot
Determination, dedication, motivation
I'm talking to you, my many inspirations
When I say I can't, let you or self down
If I were of the highest cliff, on the highest riff
And you slipped off the side and clinched on to your life in my grip
I would never, ever let you down
And when these words are found
Let it been known that God's penmanship has been signed with a language
called love
That's why my breath is felt by the deaf
And why my words are heard and confined to the ears of the blind
I, too, dream in color and in rhyme
So I guess I'm one of a kind in a full house
Cuz whenever I open my heart, my soul, or my mouth
A touch of God reigns out

-J. Ivey, College Dropout

215

OUR DEEPEST FEARS

Our deepest fear is not that we are inadequate.
Our deepest fear
is that we are powerful beyond measure.
It is our light, not our darkness,
that most frightens us.
We ask ourselves, who am I to be brilliant, gorgeous,
talented and fabulous?
Actually who are we not to be?
You are a child of God.
Your playing small doesn't serve the world.
There is nothing enlightened about shrinking
so that other people
won't feel insecure around you.
We are all meant to shine as children do.
We were born to make manifest
the glory of God that is within us.
It's not just in some of us; it's in everyone.
And when we let our own light shine,
we unconsciously give other people
permission to do the same.
As we are liberated from our own fear,
our presence automatically liberates others.

- Marianne Williamson

WORDS TO LIVE BY

"A people without knowledge of their past history, origin and
    culture is like a tree without roots."
    -Marcus Garvey

"Education is the passport to the future, for tomorrow belongs
    to those who prepare for it today."
    -Malcolm X

"Complacency is the enemy of achievement." -Dennis Kimbro

"You ain't a nigger because you black, you a nigger cause of how you
    act, but you don't want me to tell you the truth, so I'ma lie to
    you make it sound fly to you. The nigger experience."
    -Cee-Lo Green

"If you don't make your own choices, someone else will make a
    choice for you."
    -Dr. Abdalla Rashad Tau

"A man who won't die for something is not fit to live."
    –Dr. Martin Luther King, Jr.

"I would rather die on my feet than live on me knees."
    -Charles Houston

"For every dark night, there's a brighter day." -Tupac Shakur

"I don't care what you do in life, as long as it's not illegal or
    immoral." -Carolyn Rosemond

"If there is no struggle, there is no progress."
    -Frederick Douglass

"Don't use the word friend loosely. If you're lucky, you may have
    one true friend your whole life."
    -Bobby Lee Rosemond

"When I discover who I am, I'll be free." -Ralph Ellison

"One must talk little, and listen much." -Mauritanian Proverb

"How will you survive in life, if you refuse to prepare for it?"
    -Dr. Abdalla Rashad Tau

"A man who stands for nothing will fall for anything."
   -Malcolm X

"We declare our right on this earth...to be a human being, to be
   respected as a human being, to be given the rights of a
   human being in this society, on this earth, in this day,
   which we intend to bring into existence *by any means
   necessary*." –Malcolm X

"Freedom is never voluntarily given by the oppressor; it must
   be demanded by the oppressed." -Martin Luther King, Jr.

"An idle mind is the devil's workshop."
   -African-American Folk Saying

"Seeing is different from being told." -Kenyan Proverb

 "If you stop struggling, then you stop life."
   -Huey Newton

"By three methods we may learn wisdom: First, by reflection,
   which is noblest; Second, by imitation, which is easiest; and
   third by experience, which is the bitterest."
   -Confucius

"A man is but the product of his thoughts what he thinks, he
   becomes."
   -Mahatma Gandhi

"Emancipate yourselves from mental slavery, none but
   ourselves can free our minds!"
   -Bob Marley

"Don't believe what someone tells you at face value, always
   research the information for yourself."
   -Dr. Abdalla Rashad Tau

"I only debate with my equals, all others I teach."
   -John Henrick Clark

"I freed a thousand slaves I could have freed a thousand more
   if only they knew they were slaves."
   -Harriet Tubman

SUGGESTED READING

The Mis-Education of the Negro, by Carter G. Woodson

The Biography of Malcolm X, by Malcolm X & Alex Haley

The 48 Laws of Power, by Robert Greene

The Art of War, by Sun Tzu

King Leopold's Ghost, by Adam Hochschild

How Europe Underdeveloped Africa, by Walter Rodney

Soul on Ice, by Eldridge Cleaver

Cooked, by Jeff Henderson

Evolve Your Brain: The Science of Changing Your Mind,
    by Joe Dispenza

Letters to a Young Brother, by Hill Harper

African American Religious Thought: An Anthology, by Eddie
    S. Glaude & Cornel West

God the Black Man and Truth, by Ben Ammi

*Teaching Reading to Black Adolescent Males: Closing the
    Achievement Gap*, by Alfred W. Tatum

The Birth of a Nation, by Melvyn Stokes

War and Peace, by Leo Tolstoy

The Prince, by Niccolò Machiavelli, Thomas More, Martin
    Luther, William Roper

Race Matters, by Cornel West

The Classic Slave Narratives, by Henry Louis Gates Jr.

*Africana: The Encyclopedia of the African and African
    American Experience*, by Henry Louis Gates

*Words You Should Know in High School: 1,000 Essential
    Words to Build Your Vocabulary*, by Burton Jay
    Nadler, Jordan Nadler

Behold a Pale Horse, by Milton William Cooper

Brainwashed, by Tom Burrell

Rich Dad, Poor Dad, by Robert T. Kiyosaki

Stanley: The Impossible Life of Africa's Greatest Explorer, by
    Tim Jeal

Introduction to African Religion, 2nd Edition, by John S. Mbiti

The Four Agreements: A Practical Guide to Personal Freedom,
    by Don Miguel Ruiz

Building Your Own Life Brand, by Stedman Graham

*Black Wall Street: From Riot to Renaissance in Tulsa's
    Historic Greenwood District*, by Hannibal B. Johnson

Without Sanctuary: Lynching Photography in America,
    by James Allen, Hilton Als, Congressman John Lewis,
    Leon F. Litwack

The Red Book of Guerrilla Warfare, by Mao Zedong

Message to the Blackman in America, by Elijah Muhammad

The Black Male Handbook, by Kevin Powell

White Like Me, by Tim Wise

The Willie Lynch Letter and the Making of a Slave, by Kashif
    Malik Hassan-El

The Debt, by Randall Robinson

*Why Are All the Black Kids Sitting Together in the
    Cafeteria?*, by Beverly Daniel Tatum, Ph.D.

The Rose That Grew From Concrete, by Tupac Shakur

The Pact, by Drs. Sampson Davis, George Jenkins, and Rameck
    Hunt

W.E.B. Du Bois, by David Levering Lewis

Dreams from My Father: A Story of Race and Inheritance, by
    President Barack Obama

ACKNOWLEDGEMENTS

I would like to thank my parents for never giving up on me, even when I was going through my most delinquent stages in life. My mother always said that I was going to make a great adult, but I was a horrible child.

REFERENCES

Alder, F., Mueller, G., & Laufer, W. (2007). *Criminology*. Boston: McGraw Hill.

Bernburg, J. G. (2002). Anomie, social change, and crime: A theoretical examination of institutional-anomie theory. *British Journal of Criminology, 42*, 729-742.

Broidy, L. M. (2001). A test of general strain theory. *Criminology, 39*, 9-35.

Donnelly, M. S., & Straus, M. A. (2005). *Corporal punishment of children in theoretical perspective*. New Haven: Yale University.

Featherstone, R., & Deflem, M. (2003). Anomie and strain: Context and consequences of Merton's two theories. *Sociological Inquiry, 73*(4), 471-489.

Heckert, A., & Heckert, D. M. (2004). Using an integrated typology of deviance to expand Merton's anomie theory. *Criminal Justice Studies, 17*(1), 75-90.

Hirschi, T. (1969). *Causes of delinquency*. Berkley, CA: University of California Press.

Ivey, J. (2004). Never let me down [Recorded by K. West]. On *The College Dropout* [CD]. New York: Rock-A-Fella Records.

Merton, R. K. (1938). Social structure and anomie. *American Sociological Review, 3*(5), 672-682.

Messner, S. F., & Rosenfeld, R. (2001). *Crime and the American dream* (3rd ed.). Belmont, CA: Wadsworth.

Passas, N. (2000). Global anomie, dynomie, and economic crime: Hidden consequences of neoliberalism and globalization in Russia and around the world. *Social Justice, 27*, 16-44.

Tittle, C. R., & Paternoster, R. (2000). *Social deviance and crime: An organizational and theoretical approach.* Los Angeles, CA: Roxbury.

Wagner, M., Dunkake, I., & Weiss, B. (2004). Truancy: An empirical analysis of the deviant behavior of pupils]. *Kölner Zeitschrift für Soziologie und Sozialpsychologie, 56,* 457-489.

Williamson, M. (1996). *A Return to Love: Reflections on the Principles of A Course in Miracles.* New York: HarperCollins

Emancipation through Education and Exposure

Made in the USA
Charleston, SC
03 February 2012